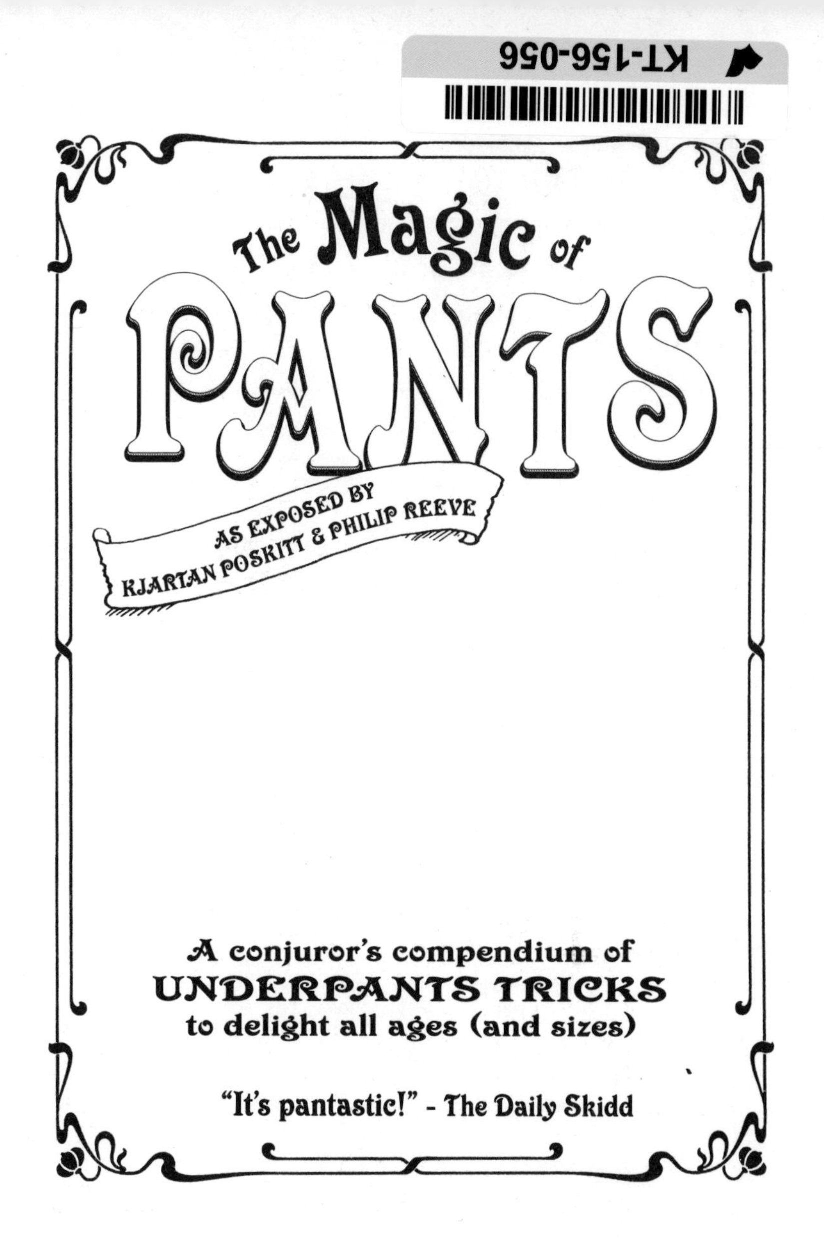

The Magic of
PANTS
AS EXPOSED BY
KJARTAN POSKITT & PHILIP REEVE
A conjuror's compendium of
UNDERPANTS TRICKS
to delight all ages (and sizes)
"It's pantastic!" - The Daily Skidd

HONI SOIT QUI MAL Y PANTS

MR REEVE

To my brother Tom
and his unforgettable pants

Scholastic Children's Books,
Commonwealth House, 1–19 New Oxford Street,
London WC1A 1NU, UK

A division of Scholastic Ltd
London ~ New York ~ Toronto ~ Sydney ~ Auckland
Mexico City ~ New Delhi ~ Hong Kong

Published in the UK by Scholastic Ltd, 2004



Go to www.magicofpants.co.uk

ISBN 0 439 96860 7


Printed and bound by AIT Nørhaven A/S, Denmark

2 4 6 8 10 9 7 5 3 1

# Contents

**Street Tricks**



**Theatre Tricks**



**Designer Tricks**

**Showstoppers**

# Warning

Before we start seeing the tricks and how they work, remember:

A MAGICIAN MUST NEVER REVEAL HIS SECRETS*

*Unless of course he is writing a book of magic tricks, in which case he can reveal everything. But even though it's quite all right for a magician writing a book to reveal his secrets, what is NOT all right is if the reader tells everybody how all the tricks work because then nobody else would bother buying the book and the magician wouldn't get any more money. That is why in every magic book ever written, somewhere, you'll find this stern warning:

A MAGICIAN MUST NEVER REVEAL HIS SECRETS

# The Origin of Pant Magic

It was exactly 96 years ago today that a little-known conjuror – *The Great Gusset* – was on board a ship bound for the distant province of Grand Thong. He had been invited to perform for the Empress but just as the coastline came into view on the horizon, tragedy struck. The ship hit a large rock and immediately sank, taking the conjuror's trunk of magical apparatus with it. Despite being the sole survivor, Gusset was determined to fulfil his engagement, so he boldly swam ashore clutching the only item he could salvage – his overnight suitcase.

That very evening he appeared in front of the court and, with breathtaking ingenuity, he performed an astounding display of illusions, tricks and marvels. But the most remarkable aspect of the presentation was that it was entirely based around the contents of his case – 17 pairs of pants.

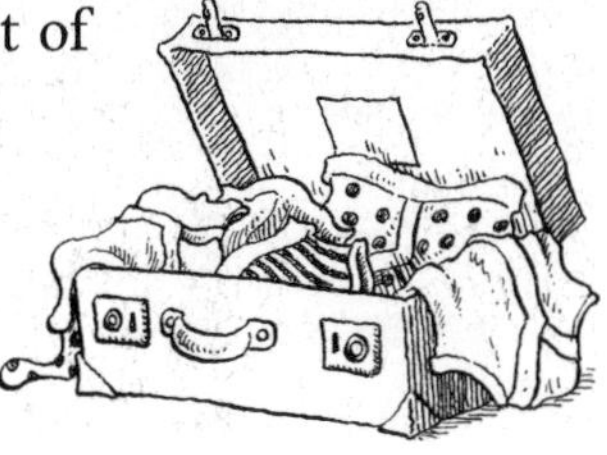

The mysteries of his perplexing pants have been closely guarded for many years, but now at last the secrets of his underwear are to be exposed. Whether you wish to re-enact the horrors of *Escape from Pantzatraz,* startle your friends with your own double-bottom pants, impress them with your mastery of the "Gusset Release" or simply charm everyone with *The Unexpected Undies,* you can now perform these feats and many more in the safety and comfort of your own pants.

## How to Use This Book

Each trick has been given a rating as to the skill required for preparation and performance. This rating is not linked to the amount of preparation, but purely to the level of technical expertise required.

**▼ = easy ▼▼ = medium**
**▼▼▼ = hard ▼▼▼▼ = ridiculous**

The tricks in this book are divided into six sections. It is suggested that beginners work through the tricks in the order in which they are presented here.

**INTIMATE TRICKS:**
*suitable for performance to an informal audience of just a few persons or even a single individual.*

**PARTY TRICKS:**
*suitable for a gathering of between five and fifty persons.*

**STREET TRICKS:**
*suitable for performance in shopping centres, on station platforms or in public car parks.*

**THEATRE TRICKS:**
*suitable for stage performance.*

**DESIGNER TRICKS:**
*require the use of more complicated props, thus allowing you to display your artistic and creative skills.*

**SHOWSTOPPERS:**
*three spectacular pant tricks requiring assistants, costumes and stage technicians.*

The book also contains a selection of special features:

**PANT PRACTITIONER'S GUIDES:**
*these are features on special props or techniques that you'll need to perform some of the tricks.*

**DECEIVER'S DEFINITIONS:**
*occasionally, unfamiliar words will appear. These are marked* and an explanation will be found at the bottom of the page.*

**PANTS PATTER:**
*these are interesting and informative anecdotes that you will find scattered throughout the book and may be used during a performance to amuse or even misdirect* your audience.*

Before embarking on the tricks, be sure to study the next section, which outlines some of the essential information required when attempting the magic of pants.

*Deceiver's definition: MISDIRECT – to distract your audience's attention while you perform some secret move.

## The Pant Practitioner's Guide to... BORROWING PANTS

*Some of the tricks will require the use of specially prepared pants, but otherwise whenever possible you should use pants lent to you by a spectator. It always adds to the audience's excitement when they see a pair of borrowed pants in action.*

*Care should be taken to ensure that you borrow pants from the right person. In some instances, a trick will work better with small pants, while other tricks require larger more substantial pants. As you gain experience, you will be able to assess what sort of pants a person is likely to lend you.*

*If you require large pants, the gentleman at the top of the next page would be very suitable. However, if you require small pants, then the lady on the right would be better.*

*The texture of the borrowed pants is often of importance too. For some tricks, it is important to use delicate pants with a soft silky texture, and yet other tricks require tough, heavy-duty pants. In this case, it can prove much more difficult to assess who is likely to have the correct pants for your purposes.*

*Should you require delicate silky pants, the lady on the left below will almost certainly be able to oblige. But, should you require industrial-strength working pants, you're out of luck. The gentleman on the right is also wearing delicate silky pants.*

*However it turns out that this next lady's undergarments are built to*

*withstand an artillery attack and therefore would serve the purpose admirably.*

*Be aware that some people are more reserved than others when it comes to lending their pants, and some may well refuse completely.*

*The gentleman on the left below is likely to be shy about lending his pants, so it would be wise not to ask him. Furthermore, it would be downright dangerous to ask the lady on the right.*

*Of course, most people will be delighted to lend you their pants, but care should be taken to ensure the pants are suitable for public viewing.*

*Although this gentleman would consider it an honour to have his pants borrowed, they may have been on for so long that it might be impossible to remove them without the aid of surgical instruments.*

*To be absolutely safe, one way of ensuring that you can borrow suitable pants is to provide them yourself. Offer a box of assorted pants to a member of the audience and ask them to pick a pair for you to perform with.*

*Finally, be aware that it's simply not worth asking some people if you can borrow their pants...*

*HINT: If you only have a limited time for your performance, it might be wise to suggest that spectators wear their pants outside their clothes. This will reduce the amount of time it will take them to remove their pants, and gives you the opportunity to assess what type and colour of pants they are wearing.*

# What You Need

For each trick, there's a list of any special materials or items you will need. Apart from pants, these include elastic bands, glue, paper, playing cards, scissors, screwdriver, hammer, drinking glasses, mirror, steel cable, pens, cotton, high-powered electric winches, envelopes, paint, stickers, stepladder, string, ants, needles, tape, nails and maggots.

You will probably be able to find all the items around your house. Otherwise, they should be available at your local hardware store.

(It should be noted that the Great Gusset's tricks at Grand Thong were not entirely performed with just his 17 pairs of pants. Before he started, he went round the palace and gathered up all the extra articles mentioned above but, rather curiously, he also collected two camels, a crash helmet and a small toasting fork. Sadly the exact details of how these items were incorporated into a pants trick have been lost. The only thing we do know is that, immediately after the performance, the Empress had to have her carpet cleaned.)

## The Pant Practitioner's Guide to...
## THE PRIVATE PARTS OF PANTS

*Before attempting any of the tricks in the book, it pays to be familiar with all the special components to be found in a pair of pants.*

*Here is a standard pair of gentlemen's pants. Most ladies' pants are exactly the same, but cleaner.*

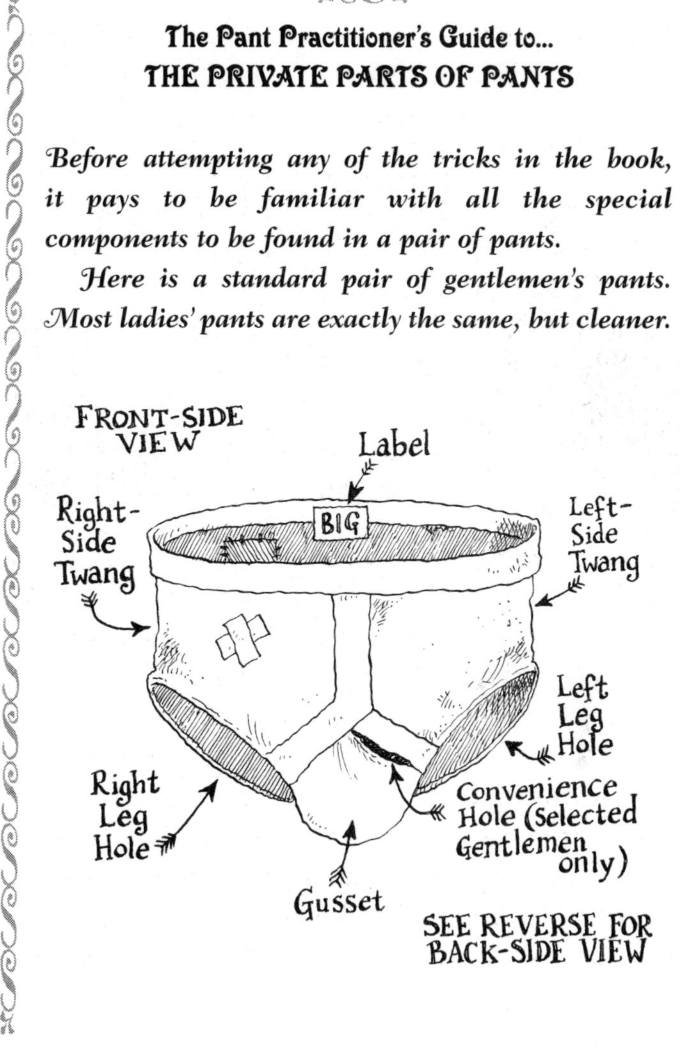

# Intimate Tricks

*Tricks suitable for small gatherings of between one and five people. Remember that even the greatest magicians started by honing their skills in front of just a few close friends, family members or fellow inmates. Also be reassured that a well-executed trick is just as magical to an audience of one as it is to an audience of one million. Although these tricks are ideal for the beginner, they are also invaluable to the professional.*

# The Power of Pants ♥

*A self-working trick* that is ideal for the beginner*

This neat little trick is ideal for those occasions when you find yourself required to entertain one or two people in a confined space.

The conjuror puts a pack of playing cards face down on the table and invites a volunteer to lift up part of the deck. The volunteer must then turn over the top card of the lower half, lay it to the side face up, then replace the top half of the deck. This may be repeated two or three times and each time a normal playing card is revealed.

*Deceiver's definition: SELF-WORKING TRICK – a trick that does not require any secret moves by the conjuror.

Finally, the conjuror invites the volunteer to remove the top part of the pack as before, but lay it face down beside the bottom half. The volunteer is then asked to lay the bottom half of the deck across the cards she just put down to mark where the cut was.

Before checking the cut card, the conjuror passes the volunteer a pair of pants to put over her head. He explains that the power of the pants will now affect the card she has already cut. The volunteer is now asked to raise the top part of the deck and turn over the card on top of the lower pile and...

The spectators may look through the rest of the pack and see that this is the only card with pants on it. Furthermore, the conjuror has not touched the cards at any time during the trick!

**WHAT YOU NEED**

- A pack of cards
- A pair of pants
- A permanent felt pen - i.e. a pen that doesn't smudge

**PREPARATION**

Take any card you like from the pack. (It doesn't need to be a complete pack.) Use the pen to draw a pair of pants on the face of the card. If it's a nice pack of cards use the joker to avoid spoiling any other cards.

**PERFORMANCE**

Put the pack face down on the table with the pants card face down on top of the pack. Make sure your volunteer follows the instructions exactly as above and the trick will work automatically.

Obviously, the volunteer will end up turning over the card that was at the top of the pack to begin with.

To distract her from realizing this, make a big fuss while she's putting the pants on her head about how powerful the pants are and how they must be worn in exactly the right way. You can even do a few magic gestures as if transferring the power of the pants down to the pack of cards.

# Ants in the Pants ♥

*Bring your lingerie to life – the perfect picnic trick*

The conjuror has a glass with a few ants in it. He takes a small pair of pants from his pocket and places them in the glass. He taps the glass to wake the ants up and then...

**PANTSACADABRA!!**

**...the pants start to twitch and even try to wriggle out of the glass.**

WHAT YOU NEED

- A glass tumbler
- A very flimsy pair of pants
- Some ants (you can either use real ants or otherwise finely chopped tea leaves look quite convincing at a distance)
- A very thin piece of black cotton thread about 50 cm long. Even better, if you have very long hair, a single strand is ideal.

PREPARATION

Tie one end of the thread to a side twang of the pants. The other end should be tied to a button on your jacket, or a pin in your clothing. Put some ants in the glass.

PERFORMANCE

Hold the glass in front of you with your left hand and drop the pants into it, keeping the thread loose. (The thread should be unnoticed by the spectators.) As you tap the glass with the fingers of your right hand, bring the glass forward so that the thread tightens and the pants twitch. For further pant movements, bring your right hand down behind the glass and secretly hook the thread with the little finger of your right

hand. By moving the glass and your right hand separately, the pants can be made to perform a range of ant-infested acrobatics.

NOTE: Instead of *Ants in the Pants* you may like to perform *Maggots in the Pants*. Substitute the ants either with real maggots or a few grains of soft-boiled rice.

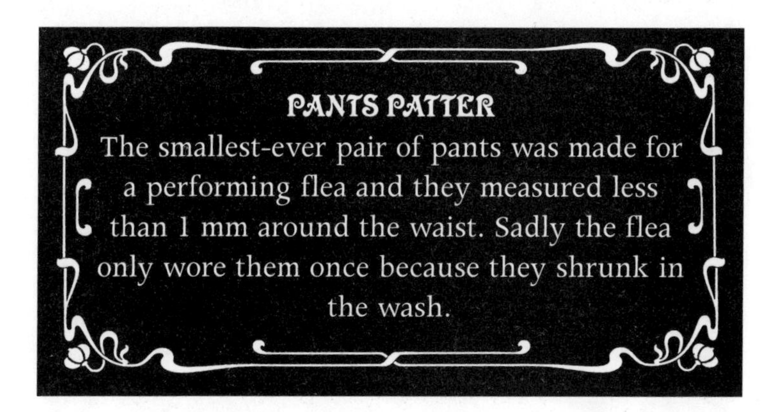

**PANTS PATTER**

The smallest-ever pair of pants was made for a performing flea and they measured less than 1 mm around the waist. Sadly the flea only wore them once because they shrunk in the wash.

# The Ringing Pants

*A table-top miracle, ideal for dinner parties*

## WHAT YOU NEED

- A pair of large pants with a label inside
- A paper clip (if possible the same colour as the pants)
- A piece of string or a shoelace about 75 cm long

## PREPARATION

The paper clip needs to be stitched to the back of the label of the pants (see diagram). When the label is folded down, the clip should be hidden.

**PERFORMANCE**

Thread the string through the leg holes of the pants and pull it tight to show it is unbroken. Then lie the string and pants on the table. The pants should be bottom side up and the waistband should be towards you. Ask your volunteer to put a finger on each end of the string. The string must be quite slack.

Put your hands with the ring into the pants via the waistband. All the next moves are performed under cover of the pants.

1. Pull a loop of string up through the ring.
2. Hook the loop on to the paper clip.

3. Take a bit of string between the clip and the ring and make it into a loop with your left finger and thumb.
4. With your right finger and thumb take a loop of string from the other side of the ring.
5. Tie these loops together as if you were just finishing tying your shoelaces. Pull the loops as tight as you can and you should end up with a simple bow tied to the ring. Bring your hands out from the pants.

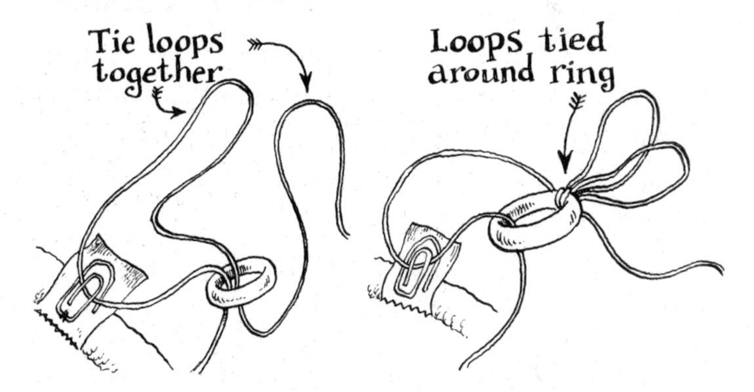


6. Ask your volunteer to let go of the string under his right finger, but to keep his left finger holding the string in place. Take the pants and with one smooth movement, pull them along and off the string. (As you do so the string will run through the paperclip and the ring, but no one else will know that.)

7. Ask your volunteer to hold up the two ends of the string and then pull the string tight. The bow will come undone and the ring will be on the string!

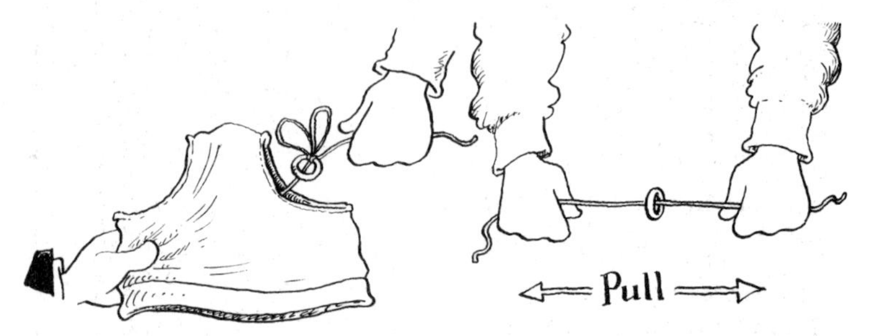


NOTE: Practise the moves without putting your hands into the pants first until you can do them with your eyes closed. And remember, you bring a loop of string through the ring before you thread the string on to the paperclip.

## The Three-pants Prediction

*A chance to force your pants*

One of the Great Gusset's most remarkable feats in the palace involved nothing more than three pairs of borrowed pants, a sheet of palace notepaper and an envelope.

When the Great Gusset asked if any of the assembled company would care to lend their undies, several dozen pairs were immediately thrust towards him. From these he asked the Empress to select any three pairs she wanted, preferably looking as different from each other as possible. The Empress chose a zebra-striped pair from the Bondelain ambassador, a glittering pink frilly pair from Queen Lulu of the Shreddie Isles and a pair of steam-driven, leather-reinforced hunting pants from the famous explorer and part-time librarian, Sir Blithery Gasper.

The Great Gusset laid these three pairs of pants on a table before the Empress, then wrote a prediction on the piece of paper. After he had sealed the paper in the envelope, he passed it to the Empress for safe keeping. Next, he asked the Empress to examine the three pairs of pants and return two of the pairs to their owners.

When only one pair remained, the Great Gusset asked the Empress to open the envelope…

**PANTSACADABRA!!**

**…on the sheet of paper was written an exact description of the remaining pair of pants!**

**EXPLANATION**

The Great Gusset's trick simply used the technique of *Forcing Your Pants* as described below. Once the three pairs of pants had been selected from the audience, the Great Gusset wrote the description of one pair on the paper. All he needed to do was force the right pants.

This trick is suitable for performance at any major royal function at the palace, but it works equally well in the laundrette with just one volunteer.

## The Pant Practitioner's Guide to...
# FORCING YOUR PANTS

***"Forcing" is a special technique used by conjurors. You give your volunteer a selection of items and ask them to choose one of them. However, with a bit of trickery you can force them to choose the item you want without your volunteer realizing it.***

***Suppose you have three pairs of pants that are spotty, striped and starry. If you want your volunteer to choose the spotty pants proceed as follows:***

NOTE: This force is simple and effective but bear in mind that you can only do it once in front of the same audience. This force is used in both *The Three-pants Prediction* and with *The X-Ray Photopants Frame,* so do not plan to do both tricks in the same performance.

IF VOLUNTEER PICKS NON-SPOTTY PAIR
IF VOLUNTEER PICKS SPOTTY PAIR
DISCARD OTHER PAIRS
TELL VOLUNTEER TO DISCARD PANTS HE IS HOLDING, LEAVING JUST TWO PAIRS TO CHOOSE FROM
FORCE COMPLETED
ASK VOLUNTEER TO PASS YOU ONE OF THE TWO PAIRS
INDICATE THE ONLY REMAINING PAIR OF PANTS...
IF YOU ARE PASSED NON-SPOTTY PANTS...
DISCARD THEM
IF YOU ARE PASSED THE SPOTTY PANTS
ASK VOLUNTEER TO DISCARD OTHER PAIR
HOLD UP THE SPOTTY PANTS
FORCE COMPLETED
FORCE COMPLETED

# A Flash in the Pants

*A cheeky little joke*

The conjuror has a pack of illustrated cards held by an elastic band. The top card shows a person wearing trousers, but the head is missing. A volunteer is asked to take a pen and draw his own head on top of the body. The conjuror removes the card and holds it with its back to the volunteer (and any spectators that might be passing). Suddenly, he glances at the card and gasps. He passes the card to the volunteer who sees that...

**...in the picture his trousers have fallen down and his pants are visible. The card may be kept as a souvenir.**

WHAT YOU NEED

- A pack of plain white cards (ask at a stationer's shop for blank business cards)
- A thick elastic band
- Glue
- Pens

PREPARATION

Cut the top card of the pack in half. On it draw the lower half of a body wearing a pulled up pair of trousers. On the second card and third card draw a body without a head with the trousers fallen down so the pants are visible.

Replace the top card on the second card so it looks like the headless body has its trousers on. The rest of the cards should all be underneath them. Wrap the elastic band around the pack so that the band goes

over the cut edge of the short card. Put a tiny trace of glue along the edge of the short card so that it sticks to the elastic band.

**PERFORMANCE**

Show the cards with the elastic band in place. Let your volunteer draw his head on the body. Hold the cards up with their backs to the audience and pull out the second card. Turn it around and show everyone that your volunteer's trousers have fallen down. Do not let anybody examine the rest of the cards too closely.

NOTE: Don't forget to draw on the third card as well as the top two. This is so that when the second card is removed, the half card left on the top of the pack is not obvious. If you draw headless trouser-dropped bodies on all the cards, your pack will last you for a long time and you will always be ready for your next performance.

**PANTS PATTER**

Some years ago, it was possible to purchase packs of disposable paper pants. Although some of the people that tried them immediately reverted to fabric underwear, there were many others who stuck to their paper pants (especially in hot weather). The best-quality paper pants were available in packs of seven and were labelled Monday, Tuesday, Wednesday, Thursday, Friday, Saturday and Sunday. The cheaper economy pack contained 12 pairs of paper pants labelled January, February, March...

## The Secret Pants Mark ♥♥

*An old favourite with a novel twist*

Everybody has seen a trick where a conjuror holds out a pack of cards face down and says, "pick a card". Somebody picks a card, looks at the face then replaces it face down. After a bit of trick shuffling and other

assorted nonsense, the conjuror proudly produces the chosen card, by which time everybody has fallen asleep. However, thanks to *The Magic of Pants,* here is a rather marvellous variation on this tired old theme...

NOW PUT YOUR CARD BACK IN FACING UPWARDS, BUT DON'T LET ME SEE THE BACK.
BUT HE CAN SEE WHICH ONE IT IS!
I CAN NOW USE THE AWESOME POWER OF THE PANTS TO FIND YOUR CARD!
RUB
RUB
IS THIS YOUR CARD?
OF COURSE IT IS.
BUT YOU HAVEN'T CHECKED. TURN IT OVER AND LOOK AT THE BACK.

## WHAT YOU NEED

- A pair of pants worn outside your other clothing
- A spare pair of pants
- Two small packs of prepared cards
- A permanent felt pen

You can make the two packs of cards from an old pack which has a few missing. The packs should have at least ten cards each and one pack should have one extra card. (Your packs might have 12 and 13 cards.) It's best if the mixtures of cards in the two packs look the same – e.g. the packs should have roughly the same number of red and black cards, and a spread of numbers. (Don't put all high numbers in one pack and low numbers in the other. Also make sure each pack has a few of each suit. It's better to avoid aces and picture cards as these tend to be more distinctive.)

Take the smaller pack and use a permanent felt pen to draw a big pair of pants on the back of each card. This pack contains the "marked cards" and the other pack contains the "unmarked" cards.

**PREPARATION**

Hide the marked cards and the spare pants down the front of your outer pants. If you're not wearing outer pants then any convenient pocket at the front of your clothing will do, or you could tuck the hidden cards into your belt under cover of your shirt. If you're wearing a kilt, pop them into your sporran.

**PERFORMANCE**

Hold out the unmarked cards face up and let your volunteer take one. (Be sure to remember what it is, e.g. five of clubs.) As the back of the card is being shown to anybody else who happens to be passing, you turn around and then secretly swap the rest of the unmarked cards for the marked cards. When you turn around don't let anybody see the back of the marked cards. Fan them out, then let your volunteer replace the card. You can give them a little shuffle as long as you don't show anyone the backs of the cards. You then give them a rub with the spare pants, pull out the picked card (e.g. five of clubs) and, just as everybody is booing, you reveal that all the other cards have the secret pants mark on the back.

# The King of Pants ♥

*A cheeky surprise*

The conjuror shows three playing cards featuring kings of different suits, and states: "a suit is no good without any pants." The volunteer is asked to remember what the three suits are. The cards are turned over so the backs are visible. The volunteer is asked to state the suit of the king in the middle.

Once she has declared the suit, the middle card is removed and is seen to have two holes in it. To ensure there's no way the card can be switched, the volunteer is invited to put two fingers through the holes. She now turns the card over…

**...it isn't a suit card, it's the King of Pants.**

## WHAT YOU NEED

- Three playing cards of different suits (preferably kings)
- A fourth playing card
- Scissors, pens, tape, white stickers

## PREPARATION

First you need to make a gimmick* card. Take one of the kings, cut it diagonally, then use a strip of tape to stick the long side on to one of the other kings as shown in the diagram. The tape should be folded underneath. Make sure the cut card does not stick out over the edge.

*Deceiver's definition: GIMMICK – a secret piece of apparatus that makes a trick work.

Next you need to prepare the King of Pants. Take the fourth playing card, and either paint the face of it white or cover it with white paper stickers. Make sure the back of the card looks normal. Cut two holes in the card, each large enough to stick a finger through, then draw the King of Pants as shown at the top of page 45.

**PERFORMANCE**

Before showing the cards to the spectator, slide the King of Pants under the flap of the gimmick card. Put the third king on top so that it covers the rest of the King of Pants.

When you first show the three kings, they should look perfectly normal. Turn the cards over, then separate them to show the two holes in the middle card. Let the spectator put her fingers through – and there you are.

# The Healing Pants

*A little trick with a little stick*

The conjuror has a normal matchstick, which he wraps in a pair of pants. He asks a volunteer to feel the matchstick through the cloth and then snap the match into two pieces. The conjuror explains that these are healing pants, and utters the magic word…

**PANTSACADABRA!!**

**…and out of the pants falls the unbroken match.**

**WHAT YOU NEED**

- A pair of lightweight pants with a double gusset, i.e. a second layer of material between the leg-holes (almost all but the very flimsiest pants have this)
- Two safety matches

PREPARATION
Make a tiny hole at the edge of the gusset and insert one of the matches so that it is hidden inside the pants.

PERFORMANCE
Wave the pants about casually to indicate there is nothing in them. Wrap the loose match in the material, but as you offer the pants to the volunteer, arrange for the loose match to be in the cloth in the palm of your hand, and make sure the volunteer feels and breaks the hidden match.

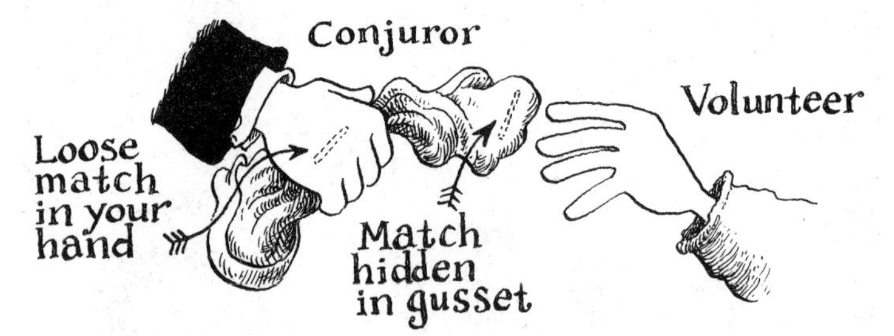


Once this is done, give the pants a little wave and let the unbroken match fall out.

# Which Undies are Underneath?

*A quaint little illusion – ideal for an impromptu* performance while sharing a table with strangers on a train*

*Deceiver's definition: IMPROMPTU – unplanned or spontaneous, done on the spur of the moment.

SEVERAL AWKWARD MINUTES LATER...
THERE...
BUT THEY'VE GOT THEIR PANTS ON THE TABLE!
HOLD YOUR PANTS IN PLACE WITH YOUR FINGER...
AND ALTHOUGH YOUR PANTS STARTED OUT ON TOP...
ROLL
ROLL

# PANTSACADABRA!!

## WHAT YOU NEED

- A pair of pants

## PREPARATION

None.

## PERFORMANCE

If possible, ensure the borrowed pants are slightly bigger than your own.

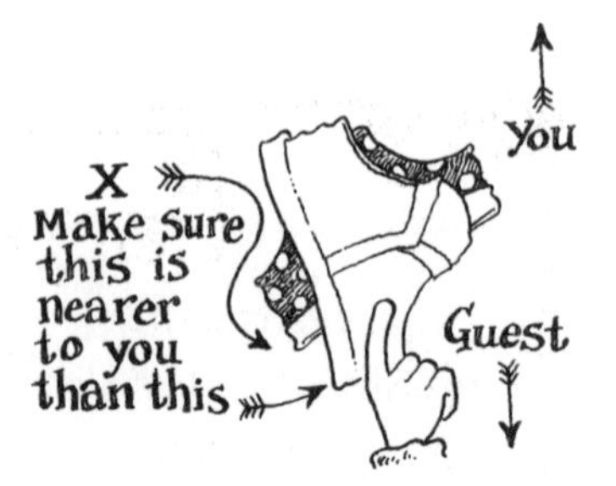


Lay the pants as shown opposite, but arrange them so that the furthest side twang of your own pants is nearer to you than the side twang of the guest pants. Roll up the two pairs of pants from your side as tightly as you can. As you approach the guest's finger, put both hands on top of the roll and give it one last push. The last bit of side twang of your own pants (marked "X" in the diagram) should flip over the roll under cover of your hand.

Quickly unroll the roll and your pants will be on top.

For maximum effect roll and unroll the pants quite quickly without pausing in the middle. A stunner.

PANTS PATTER

Despite its name, the principle export of the country of Nicaragua is coffee.

# Party Tricks

*These tricks are suitable for a larger audience, such as an after-dinner event. However, many of these tricks may be performed impromptu as a welcome diversion should an occasion warrant it. For example, if a holiday isn't going to plan, the spirits of the frustrated holiday-makers may be quickly raised by a performance of* The Knotted Knickers *or even* The Unexpected Undies.

## The Pant Practitioner's Guide to...
## DOUBLE-BOTTOM PANTS

*Before embarking on party tricks, it is time to furnish yourself with one of the most important pieces of the pant practitioner's apparatus – a special pair of gimmick* pants. It is well worth investing the time and effort required into making a pair because they are needed to accomplish several tricks that occur in this book. Furthermore, should your magical career ever dwindle to an end, they are also particularily cosy to wear on chilly winter mornings. (Just be sure to remove any hidden props such as pins, needles, daggers etc. before putting them on.)*

*To make double-bottom pants you need two identical pairs of sturdy pants.*

*Put one pair of pants inside the other and then sew them together right the way round both leg holes.*

*Carefully remove the label from the outer pair of pants, then unpick the stitching around the belt seam and remove the elastic. Stitch the label back in position (see figure 1).*

*Deceiver's definition: GIMMICK – as stated before, a gimmick is a secret device that the audience is unaware of.

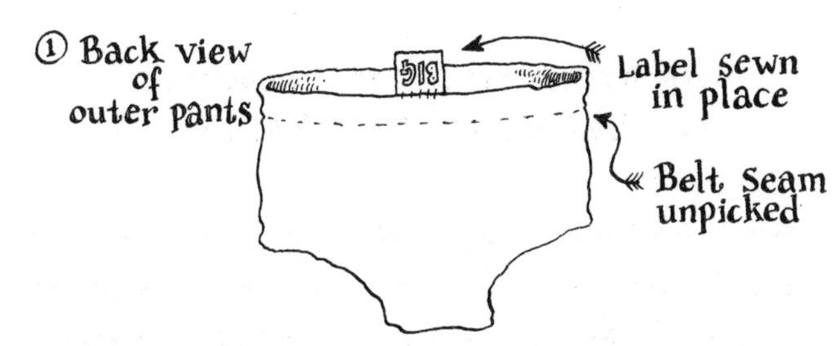


*Remove the label from the inner pants. Under where the label was (just below the belt seam) cut a slit about 4 cm long and sew around it to stop it fraying – as if making a long button hole (see figure 2).*

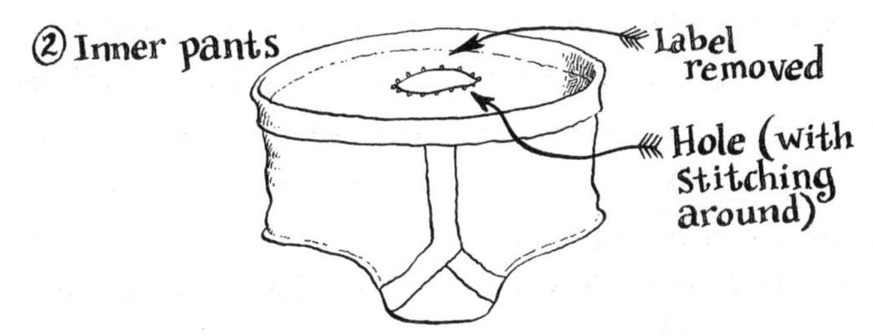


*Fold the belt seam of the outer pants over the seam of the inner pair of pants. The label should flap down across the slit in the inner pants, so helping to hide it.*

*Stitch the belt seam of the outer pants back all the way round so that the outer belt seam encloses the inner belt seam. (Your stitches will pass through both the inner and outer pants.)*

***And there you are. To anyone who is casually observing your pants, nothing will seem like it's been unnecessarily fiddled with, yet it is possible to store all manner of different items in these pants without suspicion. The pants can be removed and displayed with confidence, and then the miracles will start to happen.***

NOTE: do not undertake any of the aforementioned cutting or sewing while the pants are actually being worn.

## The Rainbow

*Your first double-bottom pants trick*

This trick was devised by the Great Gusset after he happened to be standing with the Empress on her balcony just as the monsoon rains were dripping to a finish. The sun emerged from behind a dark cloud for the first time in six weeks, and shining through the damp air it produced the most fabulous multiple rainbow. On seeing this, the Empress challenged the Great Gusset to recreate the same wondrous phenomenon with his pants.

That evening, he duly obliged. Standing before the assembled court, he explained that before a rainbow can appear the air needs to be damp. To create the right conditions, he removed his dull grey pants and, after showing them to be empty, he proceeded to wave the freshly removed pants over his head. Sure enough there was enough moisture in the pants to create the desired effect because...

**PANTSACADABRA!!**

**...to the Empress's delight, long streams of multicoloured ribbons flew from the pants in all directions.**

**WHAT YOU NEED**

- A pair of double-bottom pants
- Several brightly coloured party streamers (the ones made out of tightly rolled up paper)

**PREPARATION**

Take a few party streamers and pull about 10 cm of paper from the centre of each one. Tuck the main bit of the streamers into the secret cavity of your double-bottom pants, leaving the ends of the papers sticking out of the hole. Fold the label of the pants over the top to hide them. You may now put the pants on if you so wish.

**PERFORMANCE**

When you come to wave your pants about, hold the back of the pants with one hand and grab the ends of the streamers with the other. Move your hands apart with a flourish and the streamers will cascade from the pants.

# A Pain in the Pants

*An eye-watering illusion*

PANTSACADABRA!!
AND OUT THE BACK...
BUT IT STILL DOESN'T BURST!
WOULD ANYBODY ELSE LIKE TO PUT THE NEEDLE IN?
I RELEASE YOU FROM MY POWER!
SNAP!
PANTSACADABRA AGAIN!!
POP!

**WHAT YOU NEED**

- A pair of pants, preferably patterned
- A balloon
- A long sewing needle with about 30 cm of thread attached
- Double-sided sticky tape (this comes wrapped on a roll with a layer of protective paper to stop the tape sticking to itself)

**PREPARATION**

The balloon must be inflated so that it just fits neatly inside the pants and it is easy to slip the pants on and off.

Turn the pants inside out.

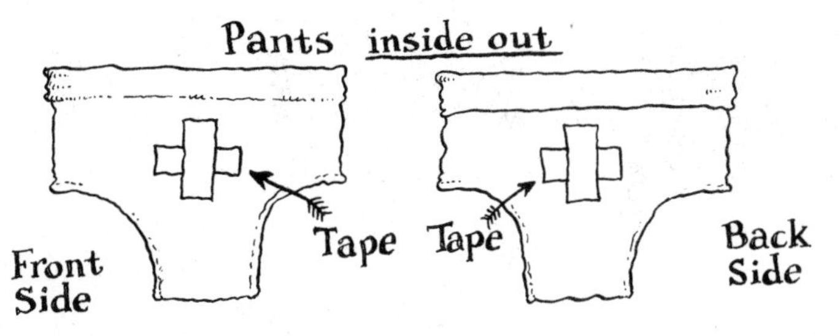


On the inside of the middle of the front of the pants you need to stick two pieces of double-sided tape in a cross. After sticking the first piece of tape, remove the protective paper then stick the second piece of tape directly across the top. Replace the piece of protective paper over the first piece of tape so that the entire cross is protected and can't stick to anything.

End of paper bent back

Bend back the very end of the protective paper on both bits of tape so that it can be peeled off quickly when required.

Put a second cross on the inside of the backside of the pants in exactly the same way, then turn the pants the right way out. From the outside there should be no sign of the tape, but you should be able to judge from the pattern on the pants exactly where the two crosses are.

**PERFORMANCE**

Show the balloon to the audience, and then pass round the needle and thread for inspection. Next you put the balloon in the pants. As you do so you must first secretly remove the protective paper from the crossed tape on the inside of the front and make sure the balloon is pushed up against the tape so it sticks. Once the front is in place, remove the protective paper from the back cross and make sure the rear of the balloon is stuck to the tape. (You can leave the loose

bits of paper wedged in between the balloon and the pants.) As this is a bit awkward, to start with you can pretend you are checking that the balloon is as comfortable as possible. Then, as you smooth the pants over the tape crosses to ensure they are stuck, you can pretend you are hypnotizing the balloon.

Ask whoever is holding the needle and thread to bring it to you. Take the needle and thread then push it through the front of the pants, making sure the needle goes through the middle of the cross! The tape will prevent the balloon from bursting. The person who brought the needle up can verify for the audience that the needle has indeed gone through into the balloon.

Next you very carefully push the needle right through so that it comes out through the middle of the back cross.

You can now hold the ends of the thread and safely swing the balloon and pants around.

Finally, pull the needle and thread right through, then click your fingers to unhypnotize the balloon. You can then invite your guest from the audience to stick the needle in it. He or she can even stick the needle in through the pants providing they miss the tape ... and the balloon will pop!

NOTES: Once you put the needle into the balloon through the tape, the balloon will start to deflate very slowly, so don't wait too long until the ending.
If possible, blow the balloon up some hours prior to performance so the rubber has time to stretch a bit. Also when blowing the balloon up, blow it further than you need and then release some air out until it is the right size. This also has the effect of reducing the tension in the rubber.

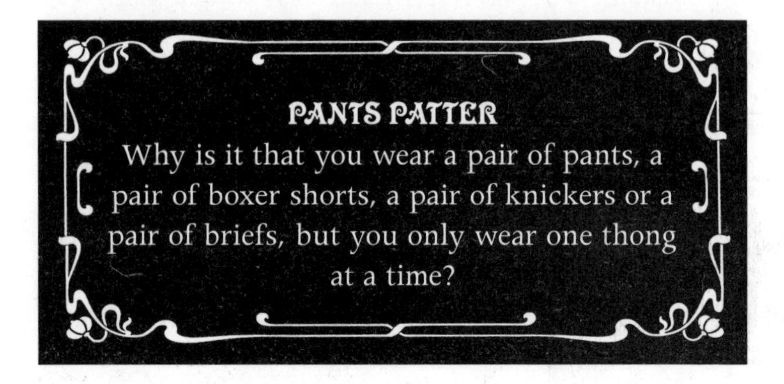

# The Knotted Knickers

*A quick, slick double trick suitable for any occasion*

The conjuror invites a lady and a gentleman to lend him their pants.

He takes the pants and tosses them up into the air, but as they come down...

**PANTSACADABRA!!**

**...the two pairs have joined together!**

He tosses them into the air again, and this time they come down unattached. Just before he passes the pants back, he puts his right arm through the leg hole of one pair of pants, and his left arm through the leg hole of the other pair "to keep them apart". Then with one swift movement he passes both pairs of pants back to the volunteers – but...

**PANTSACADABRA AGAIN!!**

**...they are knotted together!**

WHAT YOU NEED

- One small brown elastic band

PREPARATION

Wrap the elastic band tightly over the thumb and first finger of your left hand. (You may need to double the band over a few times to get it tight enough.)

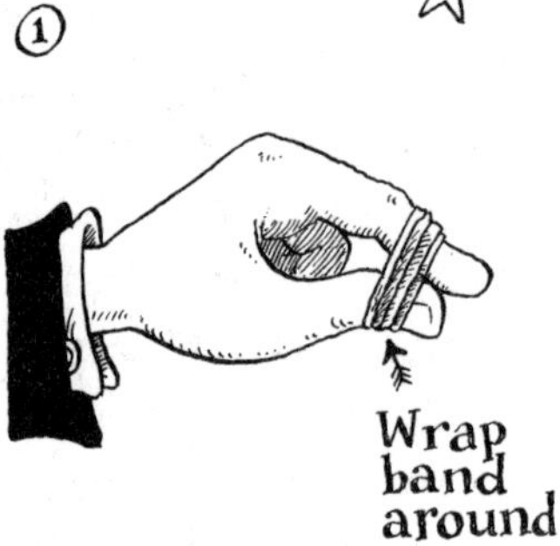

1

Wrap band around

PERFORMANCE

Try to ensure you borrow one heavy pair of pants and one flimsy pair of pants. As the pants are passed to you, take them with your right hand and then pass them over to your left hand, pushing a thick piece of the waistband between your left thumb and finger. Do this with both pairs, then bend your thumb and

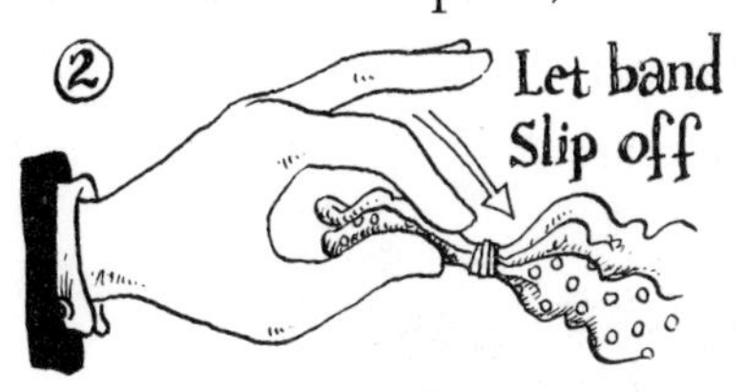


finger so that the elastic band slips off and on to the pants binding them together.

Throw them up with a gentle movement and catch the end of the heavy pair. The flimsy pair will dangle off the end. Before you throw them up again, transfer your grip so that you are holding the flimsy pair of pants. Now throw them up with a jerky movement and the band will spring away and the two pairs will separate.

Hang a pair of pants on each arm and stand between the lady and gentleman. Arrange it so that the lady is on the side of the man's pants and vice versa. Hold out your arms offering the pants to the wrong person.

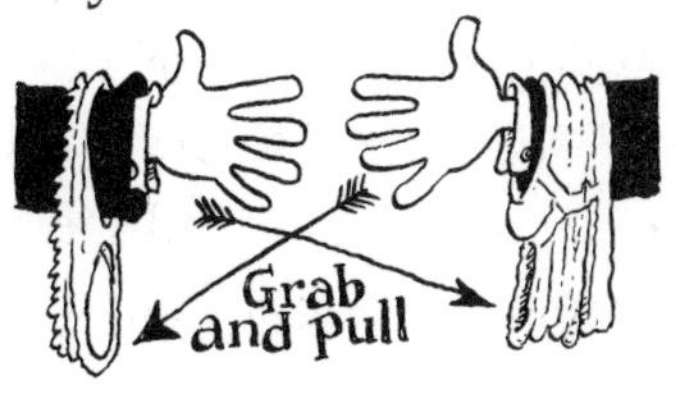

When they decline, cross your hands but, as you do so, with your left hand grab the lower section of the right pants. At the same time, with your right hand grab the lower part of the left pants. Pull the pairs of pants apart. This time the pants will be the right way round, but they will be knotted together. With practise, this can be done very quickly.

## The Unexpected Undies

*A trick to amuse absolutely everybody and fool absolutely nobody*

The conjuror holds up a long strip of paper, then folds it over a few times. A quick snip with the scissors, then he opens the paper out and...

# PANTSACADABRA!!

**...hanging on a washing line are three pairs of pants with messages on them.**

## WHAT YOU NEED

- A big sheet of paper
- Scissors
- A ruler and pencil

## PREPARATION

Draw out a strip of six equal squares on your paper and cut the strip out.

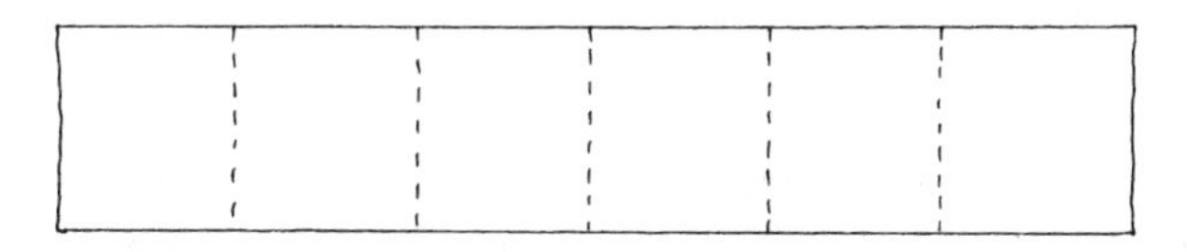

Fold the strip in and out as shown by the dotted lines. You should finish with a zigzagged strip of paper.

Draw the outline for one side of the pants on the top square of the strip. Make sure the line is the same way round as the diagram and the folded edge of the top square is to the left.

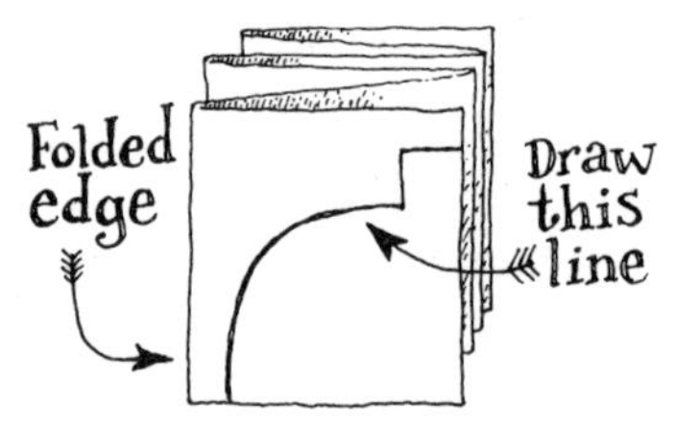


Unfold the strip of paper, then write silly names or messages or colour in the pants on the back side of the paper. (That's the side that doesn't have the outline drawn on it.) Remember that each pair of squares will cut into one pair of pants, and be sure not to write any message on a bit of paper that will be chopped out. Before you appear at the Royal Variety Performance, it's worth having a few practice goes first.

Fold your paper up so that any messages or colouring are tucked inside.

**PERFORMANCE**

Briefly open up the strip of paper to show what it is, then fold it up again. If you've written messages or done any colouring, make sure you only show the blank side of the paper. Cut carefully along the outline you drew, going through all six layers of paper. When you open the strip out, the three pairs of pants will appear. Just make sure the side with the colour or messages is facing the audience.

**MESSAGE SUGGESTIONS**

You can use this trick to convey messages in a variety of different situations.

# The Giant's Pants

*A surprising follow-on to* The Unexpected Undies

Just about everybody knows the story of Jack and the Beanstalk, where Jack climbs a beanstalk, breaks into a giant's house, steals all the giant's things and then kills him. Sadly the story as we know it has two bits missing. One bit is when everybody realizes that Jack is a trespassing, burgling murderer and is sent to jail for ever. The other missing bit is when the giant climbs down the beanstalk and secretly hangs his

pants on Jack's washing line. This forms the basis for a rather cute trick.

The conjuror shows the audience a long strip of paper that has been folded over a few times. With a pair of scissors, he chops a little section from the folded paper and opens it up to show he's made a little washing line with three pairs of pants on it. But...

**WHAT YOU NEED**

- A big sheet of paper (preferably A3 or bigger)
- Scissors
- A ruler and pencil

**PREPARATION**

Draw out a grid of equal squares on your paper – it should be seven squares long and two squares high. If you are drawing along the long side of an A3 piece of paper, each square should measure 6 cm x 6 cm.

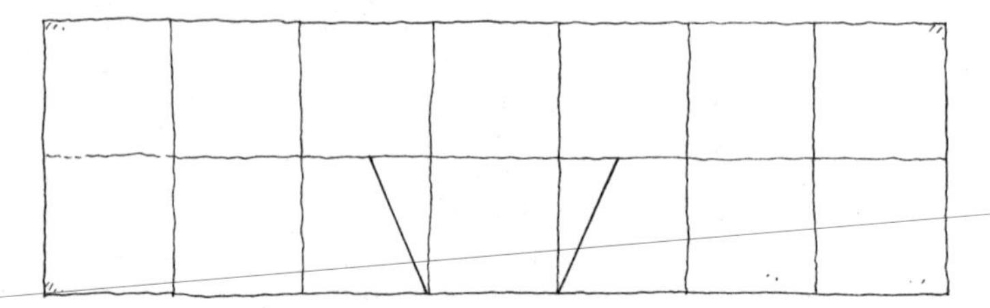

Draw in the two slanting lines as shown in the diagram. Then cut out the shape with the long strip of squares at the top and the extra bit at the bottom.

At this point, you can write something in the middle of the strip. If you're telling the giant story, you can write "Giant's Pants", or if you've got a jolly friend called Betty, maybe you'd like to put "Betty's Pants". Or you can simply colour this area in a bright colour.

Fold the extra bit up so it lies on top of the main strip.

Now fold the whole strip exactly in half, so that the extra bit is tucked inside. (See where it says "first fold" on the diagram opposite.)

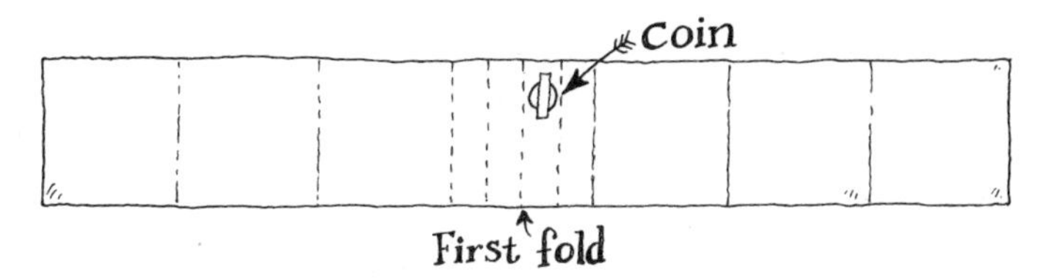


NOTE: To help the Giant Pants appear later on, you can tape a small coin on the extra flap of paper just to the side of the first fold.

Now fold the strip backwards along the two lines either side of the middle fold.

Fold the strip forwards along the next two lines, then fold it backwards along the next two lines, and finally forwards again along the last two lines. When you've finished, from the top your strip should look like this:



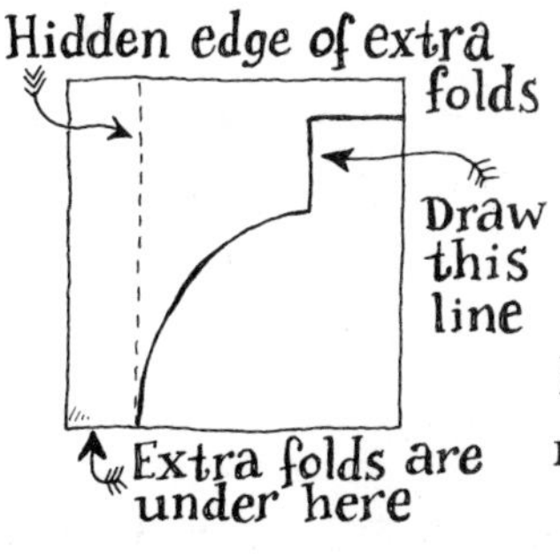


Finally, draw the outline for one side of the pants on the top square of the paper. The secret extra folds should be tucked under the left-hand side and the line should not go over them.

**PERFORMANCE**

Cut carefully along the outline you drew going through all the layers of paper. When you open the

strip out, give it a shake and the middle flap should drop down, making a pair of Giant Pants in the middle.

## The Cutting-a-pair-of-pants-in-half Trick

*A variation on the classic all-time-favourite illusion*

For many years, conjurors have been entertaining audiences with the Sawing-a-lady-in-half Trick, but by now the secret of the original illusion is too well known to perform.

This old crowd pleaser relied on having a nimble assistant who could curl up inside the box. Sadly, such ladies were deterred from helping with the trick after this unfortunate article appeared in *The Conjuror's Chronicle*:

MISGUIDED MAGICIAN ON MURDER CHARGE



Happily, there is now a new version of sawing-in-half which is every bit as exciting. But, instead of expecting a lady to agree to be sawn in half, all she is required to do is lend you her pants.

The conjuror borrows Patsy's pants and slides them through an empty toilet roll. The pants are clearly seen sticking out from either end. He then takes a large pair of scissors and cuts right through the middle of the roll. He pulls the two parts of the roll away but...

**PANTSACADABRA!!**

**...the pants are still in one piece!**

WHAT YOU NEED
- A large pair of scissors
- A specially prepared empty toilet roll (see below)

PREPARATION
Carefully make two slits in the roll as shown in the diagram. The slits should be about 3 cm apart and should each go halfway round the tube.

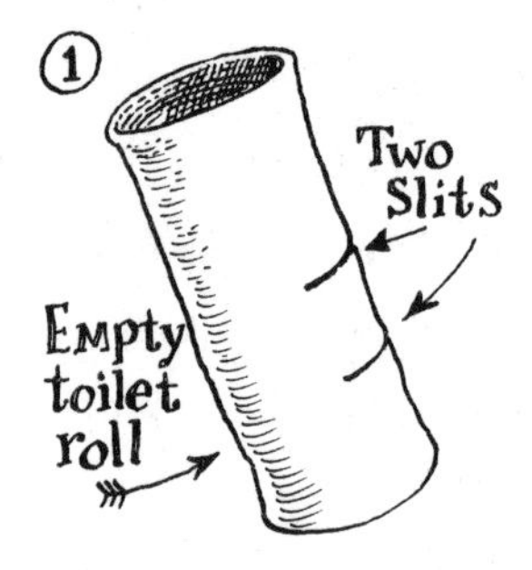


PERFORMANCE
Your audience should be in front of you. Show the tube to be empty, but keep the slits turned away from them. Borrow some pants, but then as you start to put

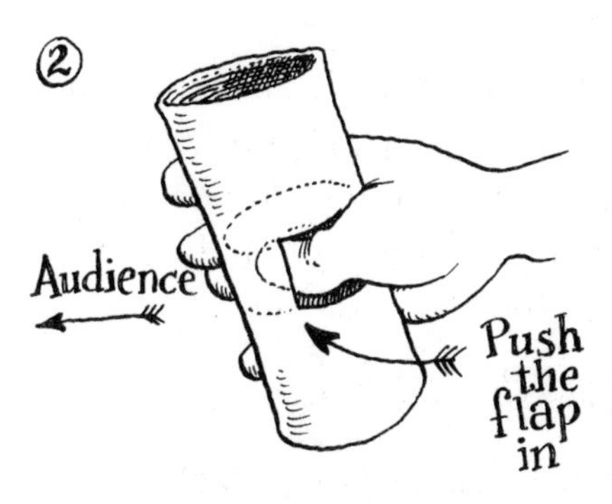


them into the roll, secretly use your thumb to push the middle of the roll across to the other side.

Bring the pants through and out of the other end of the roll. Take the scissors and feed the narrow blade between the pants and the front of the roll. Try to do this in a smooth action – it helps if you squash the roll flat and allow the pants to bulge out of the hole at the back.

Keep the front of the roll towards the audience and chop through the double layer of cardboard. Take away the scissors, then quickly pull the ends of the roll apart and discard them so that nobody notices the extra cuts and the folded section.

PANTS PATTER
If a thong is rotated and turned inside out in every possible direction, there are six possible ways in which it might be worn.
Inside out
Rotate
Rotate

# Street Tricks

*These tricks are especially suitable for outdoor performances where you can catch the public unawares.*

# The Trapped Twangs

*A marvellous little trick that will cause much gleeful embarrassment* – sponsored by Pexton's Hardware Supplies

**The fingers let go and the string is one continuous piece.**

**WHAT YOU NEED**

- A piece of normal string about 2 m long (available from Pexton's Hardware Supplies)

**PREPARATION**

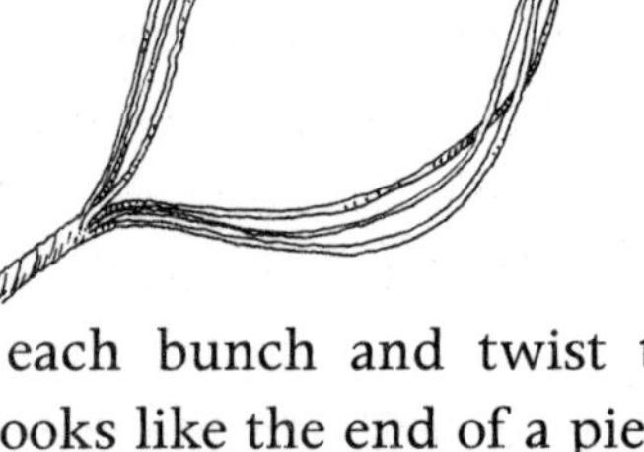


1. At the centre of the string, pull about 16 cm of the strands apart and divide into two equal bunches.
2. Take the centre of each bunch and twist them together to make what looks like the end of a piece of string. (You should find the twist in the fibres makes them naturally bond together.) You should end up with two 8-cm dummy ends of string sticking out of the middle of your continuous piece.

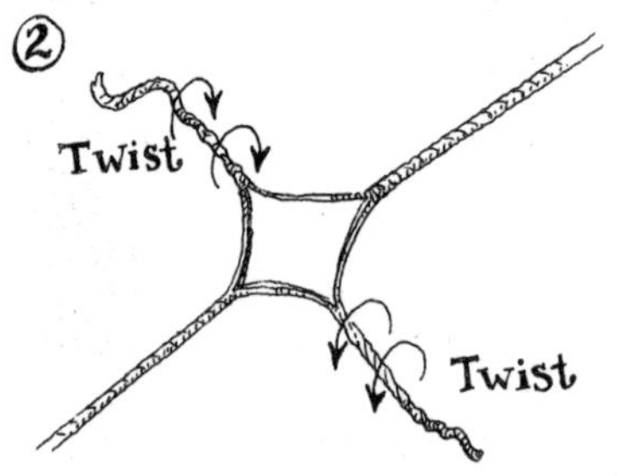


3. Always hold the string so that you have your thumb over the point where the two dummy ends come out. That will stop them untwisting and also hide the join.

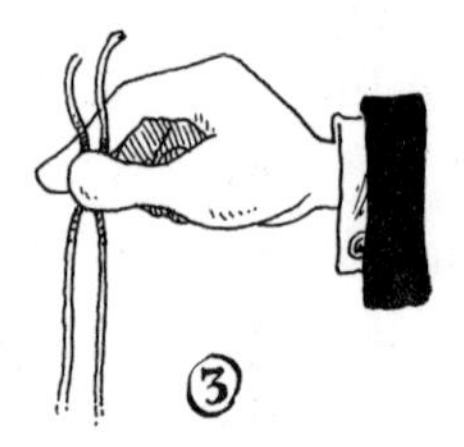

**PERFORMANCE**

Hold the string at the join with the long ends dangling down and the dummy ends sticking upwards. Be sure to mention that you have two strings. As your guests are pulling their side twangs out, take the two dummy ends with your thumbs and fingertips, make two loops, then tie them together into a little bow as if finishing tying your shoelaces. Do this quickly so that nobody notices anything strange. The bow should not be too tight.

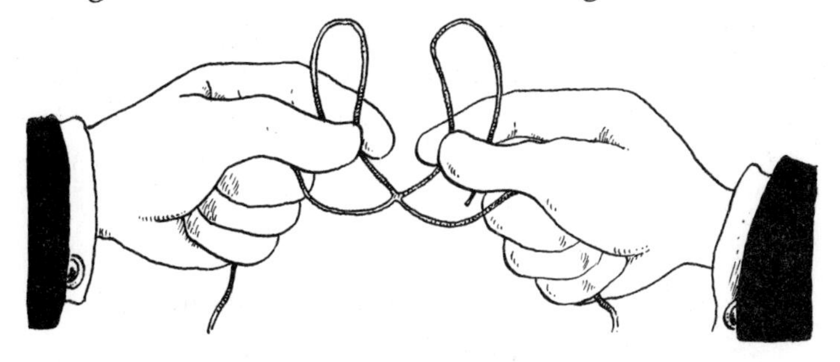

Ask your guests to each thread a long end of string through their side twangs. Make sure they are standing close enough so that the string is slack, then let the bow drop. This frees your hands to tie the two long ends together with a very secure, tight knot.

Pick up the centre of the bow between your left finger and thumb and, using your right hand, pull the bow undone. Everybody will think that you are holding two unnconnected ends of string. Explain that if you don't release the two ends of string, the side twangs of their pants will be trapped together for ever – and wouldn't that be embarrassing?

Ask your guests to step apart so that the string becomes tight, then slowly open your hand wide. The two ends will be released and disappear – one continuous piece of string will be all that is left and your hand will be seen to be empty. Your guests have been caught by Trapped Twangs.

## The Burrowed Pants ♥♥♥

*A shock in the shopping bag – a trick equally suitable for the stage or the supermarket checkout*

WE DON'T KNOW!
IF YOU LEND ME YOUR PANTS, THEY WILL BE 'BORROWED'.
WHAT DULL PANTS SHE HAS!
HERE YOU ARE THEN.
I'LL JUST POP THEM IN HERE...
DISTINCTIVE PLOP OF PANTS IN SHOPPING BAG
AHA! THEY'VE DISAPPEARED. THAT'S BECAUSE THEY'VE TURNED INTO 'BURROWED' PANTS!
RUMMAGE
SEE? THERE'S NO SIGN OF THEM. YOU CAN CHECK THE BAG IF YOU LIKE.
BUT THEY'RE THE ONLY PAIR I'VE GOT!
UNSLICED LOAF
NEVER FEAR. IF I UNWRAP THIS LOAF OF BREAD.
UNSLICED LOAF

## PANTSACADABRA!!

**WHAT YOU NEED**

- A large carrier bag
- An unsliced loaf of soft bread
- A plastic bread wrapper – the sort that has a "tie" at the end
- An empty toilet roll
- A full toilet roll (unwrapped)
- A long thin tube of sweets. (If possible, carefully remove the wrapping and replace the sweets with a solid round piece of wood, then replace the wrapper so it looks like a normal tube of sweets.)
- A few other grocery items such as a tin of beans, a carrot, cheese, tea bags, lollipops etc.
- An elastic band

**PREPARATION**

First you need to make a gimmick*. In this case, the gimmick comes from the empty toilet roll, which you're going to make slightly narrower so that it fits inside the middle of the full toilet roll. Cut the empty roll lengthways, then let the edges overlap and push it inside the full roll (see figures 1 and 2). Put 5 cm of tape down the inside of one end to hold the edges together. Pull the empty roll out again. Close up the end you haven't taped a bit more so that it's slightly narrower, then put another bit of tape down the inside of the narrow end. Finally, put some tape all the way down the outside edge (see figure 3).

Using a spoon, make a hole in one end of the loaf, just big enough to take your prepared tube. Hollow out a cavity deep inside the loaf big enough to hold a pair of pants.

*Deceiver's definition: GIMMICK – how many times do you need to be told? A gimmick is a secret device that the audience is unaware of.

Insert the narrow end of your prepared tube halfway into the back of the loaf. Pull the plastic wrapper over the loaf so that the roll sticks out of the end. Wrap the end of the wrapper around the roll and then fasten it as tightly as possible with the elastic band.

Place the loaf in the carrier bag with the open roll end sticking upwards. Put the full toilet roll upright next to it, put the tube of sweets in the centre of the full toilet roll, then finally place the other items around them.

**PERFORMANCE**

Try to ensure that the borrowed pants are a small flimsy pair. When you drop the pants down into the bag, make sure they go over the open end of the tube. Place the bag on the table with the opening upwards. Do not let anyone see into the bag.

While pretending to look for the pants, put both hands in the bag. As one hand holds the toilet-roll tube,

the other takes the tube of sweets and uses it to push the pants right down into the loaf. You can disguise what you're doing and add to the comic effect by pulling out an odd item such as the tin of beans and saying, "Is this your pants?" then replacing it.

As soon as the pants are inside the loaf, drop the sweets into the bottom of the bag, pull the tube out and let the elastic band shut the end of the bread wrapper up. Shove the tube down the middle of the full toilet roll to hide it.

Tip the items out on to the table, trying to ensure that the fastened end of the bread wrapper is away from the audience. Examine the items to make it clear that the pants are not there – and there is nothing unusual in the bag. Pick the wrapper up by the loose bit at the end, take off the elastic band and, holding your hand across the damaged end of the bread, pull the loaf out and hold it upright on your hand. Let the audience see the complete loaf for a few seconds and then completely rip it apart to produce the pants ... and at the same time disguise the fact that there was a hole in the end.

NOTE: Before starting this trick, it is wise to roll up your sleeves so that the audience is assured that you haven't sneaked the pants into the loaf while tearing it.

# Traffic-stopping Pants

*A quick-change illusion*

And as quickly as the conjuror's pants turned green, they can turn red again, with his feet hardly going out of sight! This may be repeated as often as required.

**WHAT YOU NEED**

- A loose pair of red pants
- A loose pair of green pants
- Some black ribbon
- Black velcro
- Needle and thread

**PREPARATION**

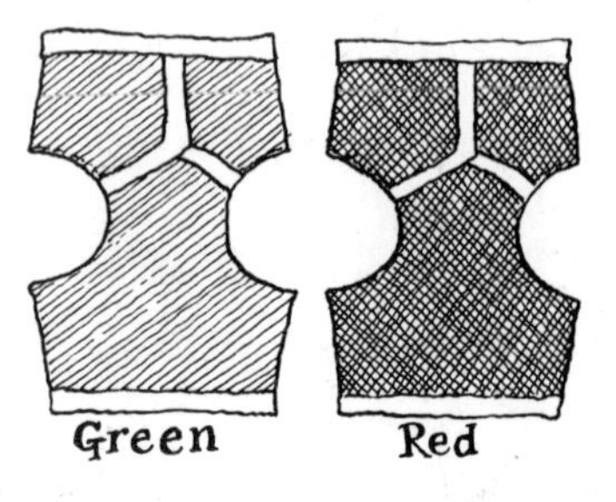


You need to make some special quick-change pants.

First take the two pairs of pants and chop them down the side twangs. You may need to stitch them up along the edges to stop them fraying.

Now use the two pieces to make a pair of pants with a red front and a green back and a red/green flap hanging down from the gusset. This is done by sewing the side twangs and gusset seam of the front of the red pants to the back of the green pants. If necessary, sew new elastic into the waistband. Next, sew the back of the red pants and the front of the green pants together all the way round.

You will probably find that the back of the pants is bigger then the front, so to disguise this you need to hem the leg holes with the black ribbon.

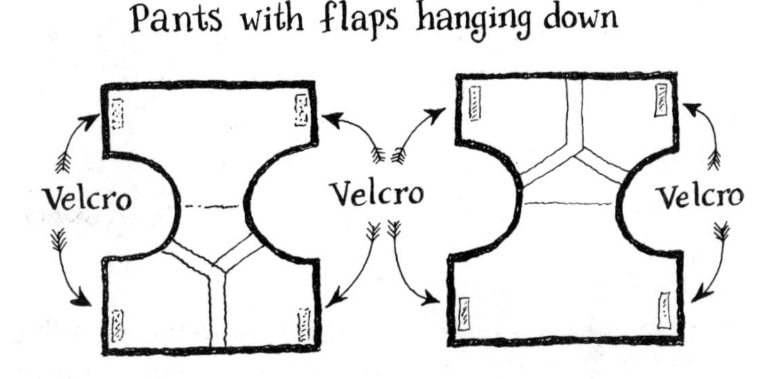


Pull on the pants, which will have a large flap hanging down from the gusset. First bring this flap forwards and up so that the green front covers the red front. Fix pieces of velcro to the side twangs of the pants and the flap so that the flap can be held in place. Both from the front and back it will appear as if you are wearing green pants.

Next lower the flap and pull it backwards between your legs and up again so that the red back covers the green back. You will need to fix more velcro to the other side of the side twangs of the flap so that it can be held up in the rear position.

Stand in front of a mirror and practise switching the flap from front to back so that you can do it very quickly.

## PERFORMANCE

Simply step behind a pillar box, then quickly swap your pants flap from front to back or vice-versa. If there is no pillar box available, this trick can be performed behind a tree or any other item that's slightly wider than your body.

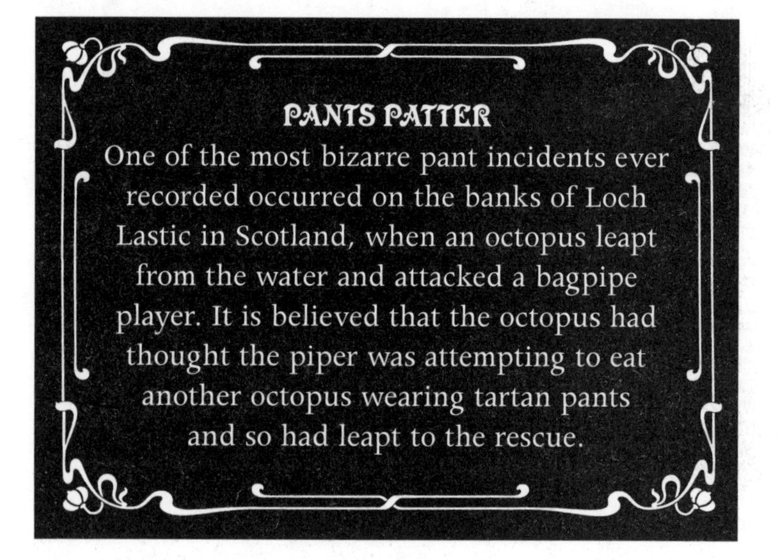

### PANTS PATTER

One of the most bizarre pant incidents ever recorded occurred on the banks of Loch Lastic in Scotland, when an octopus leapt from the water and attacked a bagpipe player. It is believed that the octopus had thought the piper was attempting to eat another octopus wearing tartan pants and so had leapt to the rescue.

# The Knicker Nicker ♥♥

*A quick escape*

This trick was invented by the Great Gusset in rather a hurry. He had been browsing in the foundation-garment department of Marks and Skids and quite absent-mindedly stepped out past the store detective with his arms still through the leg holes of a pair of big pants. Immediately the detective assumed he was nicking the pants and slapped a pair of handcuffs on the Great Gusset's wrists to preserve the evidence. The unfortunate conjuror was then shut in a changing cubicle until a police wagon arrived to convey him to the nearest magistrate.

The store detective was delighted to have apprehended such a prestigious personality, but when the police arrived and the cubicle was opened, they were met with a shock.

GUSSET GIVES PANTS THE SLIP

The Great Gusset's remarkable trick can be recreated using a pair of pants, a piece of rope and a volunteer.

The conjuror takes the pair of pants and puts one arm through each leg hole. The volunteer ties one end of the rope around one of the conjuror's wrists, and then ties the other end around the other wrist.

It seems the pants are trapped but amazingly the conjuror turns around and then in seconds he turns back and...

**PANTSACADABRA!!**

**...he tosses the released pants up in the air, even though his wrists are still tied!**

The pants may be closely inspected afterwards for anything suspicious.

**WHAT YOU NEED**

- A pair of pants
- A piece of rope (or better still, handcuffs if you have them)

**PERFORMANCE**

Slide an arm through each leg hole of the pants, then ask your volunteer to tie the rope round each wrist. The rope should be knotted tight enough so that it cannot slip over the hand, but not too tight. (You don't want your hand going blue.) It should be just loose enough so that it is possible to insert a couple of fingers between the loop and your wrist.

Turn around so that your hands cannot be seen – or if you do this trick after dinner, you can put your hands under the table. (With practice you should be able to do this trick without looking.) The strange bit is how little time it takes to remove the pants and leave the rope in place once you've mastered *The Gusset Release*.

**The Pant Practitioner's Guide to...**
**THE GUSSET RELEASE**

***Using your left hand, push the gusset of the pants right up inside the loop of rope around your right wrist. Then pass the gusset all the way over the top of your fingers of your right hand.***

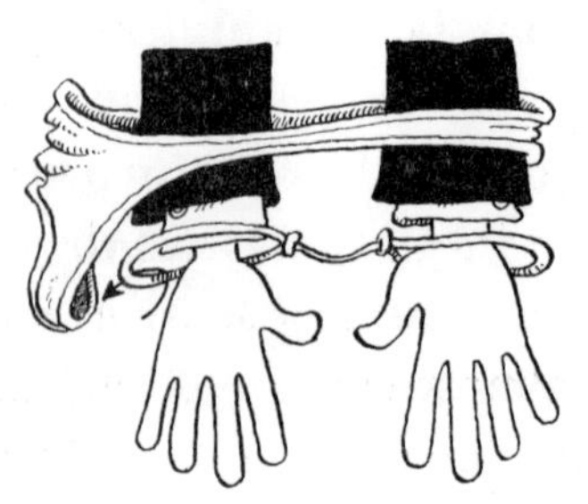

***Pull the gusset right down through the loop of rope on the other side.***

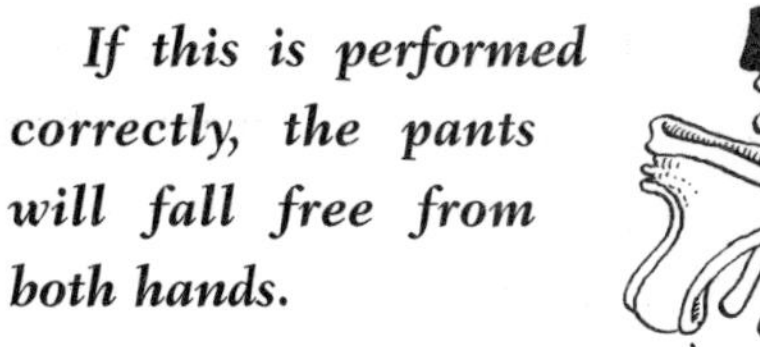

***If this is performed correctly, the pants will fall free from both hands.***

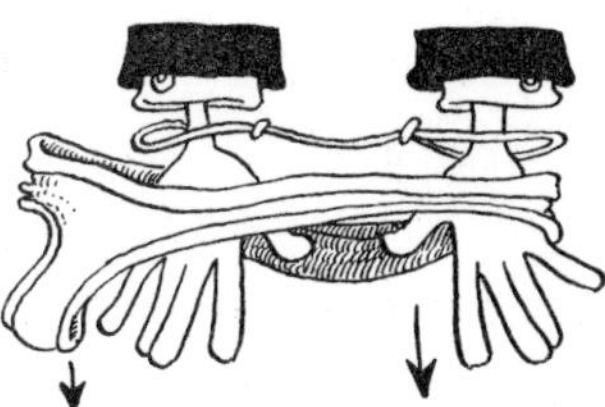

NOTE: If the pants have a particularly thick gusset or the rope loops are too tight, it may be easier to remove the pants using *The Side Twang Release,* which is featured on page 139.

## Houdini's Pants

*There's no holding these undies...*

In an effort to save the environment, all sorts of different materials are recycled, including paper, glass, tin cans and the cloth from pants. Therefore you may be curious to know what happened to the pants worn by the great escapologist Houdini. The answer is that over the years the material of his pants was shredded and mixed in with other material to make more pants, and in turn they were shredded and made into more pants and so on. By now, it is fair to assume that almost every pair of pants in the world contains a tiny element of Houdini's original pants and so we

can expect them to display some of the skills of the master himself...

...AND THEN I PASS IT TO YOU...
OOH! MY PANTS ARE WELL AND TRULY TRAPPED NOW!
OOOH!
FANCY!
AHA! YOU SHOULD NEVER UNDERESTIMATE THE INGENUITY OF PANTS.
PANTSACADABRA!!
BECAUSE NOW YOUR PANTS ARE FREE, YET THE GLASS IS STILL INTACT!
OH, SO IT'S THAT SORT OF FREE PANTS.

**WHAT YOU NEED**

- A cylindrical glass tumber (i.e. with a round bottom and sides that go straight up)
- A large cloth
- An elastic band
- A pen

**PERFORMANCE**

After your volunteer has marked her pants, jam them into the glass so that they will not easily fall out. Here comes the secret move:

Holding the glass in your left hand and the cloth in your right, bring the cloth round in front of the glass so that nobody can see the glass or your left hand. Then, as you bring the cloth over the top, turn the glass upside down. With the first finger and thumb of your right hand pull the cloth down tight over the "top" of the glass and hold it while you put the elastic band around it with your left. Then pass it to your volunteer, making sure she holds the glass by the sides.

All that remains to be done is to reach up under the cloth and inside the glass and remove your volunteer's pants. As you pass the pants back, take the glass and cloth back. Remove the elastic band and allow the glass to roll from the cloth into your hand, so disguising that it was upside down.

NOTES: When first turning the glass over, try to move your hand from the wrist and avoid moving your arm. This is easier if you are holding the glass up in front of your face.

If your hand is big enough, you might like to try a less obvious way of inverting the glass. Hold the glass at the bottom between your finger and thumb. As you bring the cloth over it, release the pressure slightly, allowing the glass to swing downwards. Then you can secure the cloth across the bottom end in the usual way.

# The Plaited Pants

*A big-scale version of the table-top ring-release trick*

The conjuror invites beween ten and fifteen people to throw their pants at him. Very quickly he plaits all the pants together to form a long rope. Then he invites two volunteers to hold either end of the rope.

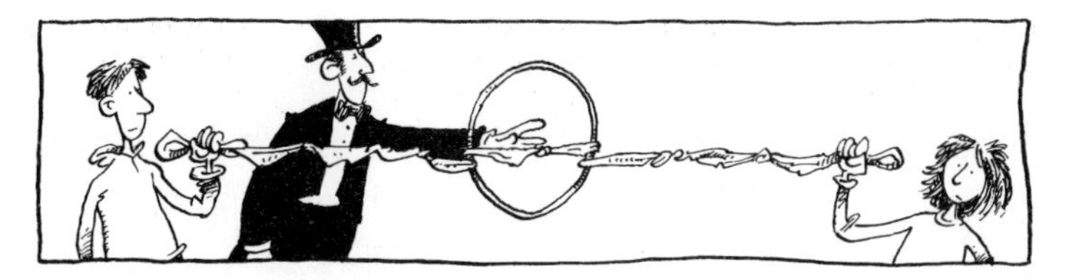

The conjuror takes a hula hoop and passes it over the rope, giving it a twist to secure it.

He then takes the end of the rope and passes it through the hoop again to secure it even more. The two volunteers at each end pull the rope tight. It seems the hoop is held fast but the conjuror tugs at it and...

**PANTSACADABRA!!**

**...the hoop comes free, yet the rope is still intact!**

**WHAT YOU NEED**

- A normal hula hoop (this may be inspected by the audience)

**PRACTICE**

Before trying this trick with an audience, practise with a piece of string and a solid ring. It helps if you can get someone to hold the string for you. These diagrams show what happens.

First put the string through the ring.

Keeping the string tight, twist the ring once.

Still keeping the string tight, pull it around the opposite side of the ring and pull it through so that it looks exactly like this:

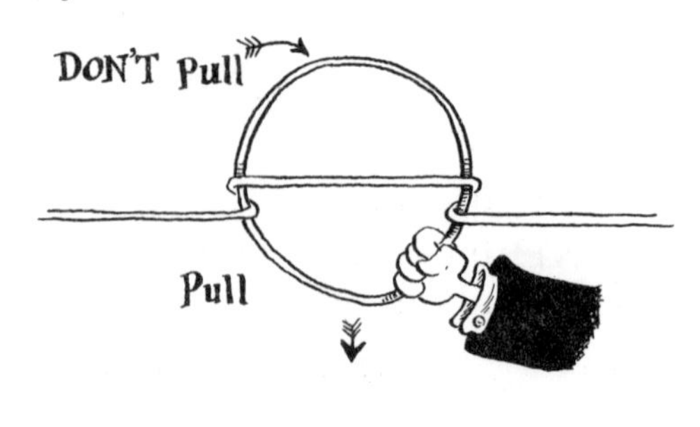

Finally, pull the ring downwards and it will come off.

You should also practise plaiting some old pants together to make the "rope".

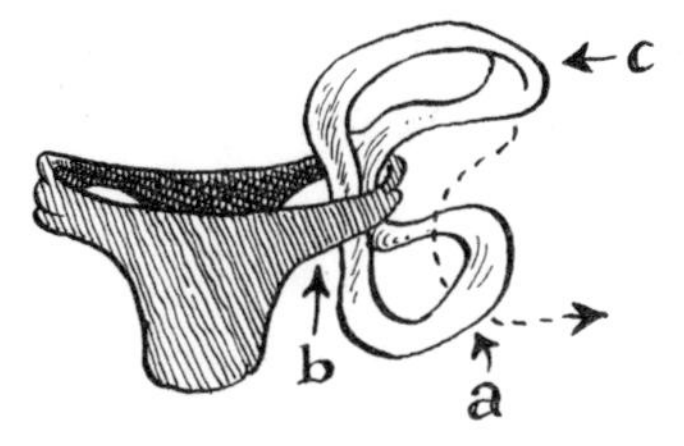


To start: put the leg hole (a) of the white pants halfway through the leg hole (b) of the black pants. Then feed the rest of the white pants (c) through the leg hole of the white pants at (a).

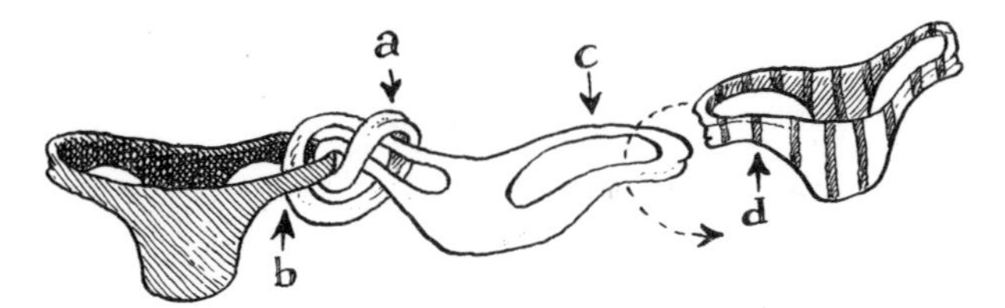


The leg hole (c) is now pulled tight to secure the white pants to the black pants, thus completing the first link of the rope. To continue, the side twang of striped pants (d) may be inserted through the leg hole of the white pants at (c) and then the rest of the striped pants passed through leg hole (d) and pulled tight, and so on.

## PERFORMANCE

The trick is performed exactly as outlined above. First you make your rope of linked pants, then thread the hula hoop on to the rope in exactly the same way as you put the ring on the string. Once you've completed both the twists, make sure the section of rope between them goes across the centre of the hoop. Make sure you grab the right section of the hoop, and then pull it away.

NOTE: This is a very easy trick and, although it looks fairly obvious when you practise with string and ring, having a long plaited line of pants disguises the simplicity of the twists.

# Emergency Pants

*Whether you wish to perform this trick on the stage or simply keep it for emergency use, it's always handy to know how to produce your own emergency pants from an innocent-looking sheet of newspaper*

## WHAT YOU NEED

- A newspaper (it's best if it's one of the smaller tabloid papers – not the broadsheets)
- A pair of lightweight pants
- Glue

**PREPARATION**

Take two sheets of the newspaper (preferably with lots of coloured pictures on them) and glue them together right round the edge, except for one opening (see diagram). Make sure that the two sheets are exactly on top of each other. If you make sure that the glue goes right to the edge of the paper, when it's dry you can trim a tiny bit off all the way round with a pair of scissors. Then when you hold the glued sheets up, they should look like one single sheet. Spread the glue extremely thinly or the paper will go wrinkly.

Slip the pants inside the two sheets of newspaper and arrange them so they are as flat as possible. Put the double sheet inside the rest of the newspaper. The newspaper can then be rolled up or folded.

## PERFORMANCE

Once you've explained that you're going to make some pants from newspaper, open the newspaper, look through it and then pull out the double sheet. Hold it by the edge where the opening is, and casually show both the front and the back. Next you need to roll the newspaper into a cone (this takes practice).

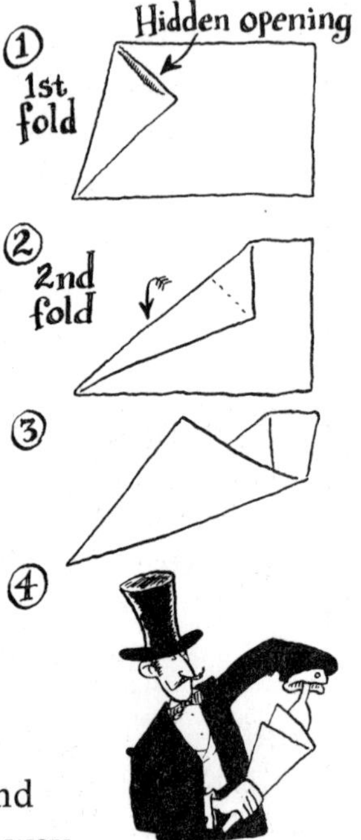


First fold over the corner by the opening, then fold the rest of the paper around it (see diagram). Then you hold the bottom of the "cone" with one hand and push your other hand inside the folds of paper. That way you can open the cone out. While you're "adjusting" the size of the cone, you can also open up the secret hole in the paper. All you do is reach inside, pull out the pants, and wave them in the air. At the same time you casually let the paper cone fall open to show there's nothing wrong with it.

# Theatre Tricks

*A theatre allows for more preparation beforehand, and as the audience is properly seated away from the stage, it is easier to control what they do and do not see. Again, some of these tricks may be performed impromptu if suitable circumstances arise.*

# Pantal Attraction ♥♥

*A strange and unnatural force*

The conjuror indicates a small sealed container set to the side of the stage. He then invites Betty on stage and asks if she can feel any strange magic force coming from the container. When Betty says that she can't feel anything, the conjuror says that they'll put the force to the test. To do this he passes her a magazine explaining that he will require her to mark one of the pages with a big cross.

He asks Betty to hold the magazine behind her back so that neither Betty nor the conjuror nor anyone else can see it. She must then open the magazine somewhere in the middle. The conjuror passes her a pen so that she can make a big cross on the open page. Finally she must close the magazine up and pass the magazine and pen back to the conjuror.

The conjuror asks Betty if she had felt particularly attracted to anything in the magazine. As he does so he flicks through the pages and shows that none of

them are marked until he finds the big cross. He asks Betty to tell the audience exactly what is pictured at the exact point where the lines cross over.

Betty states that the cross goes through a picture of some pants.

The conjuror declares that he is not surprised, because Betty was the subject of a strange force called Pantal Attraction. And where does that force come from? He asks Betty to open the sealed container and bring out the contents...

**PANTSACADABRA!!**

**...it's a pair of pants identical to the ones indicated by the cross.**

**WHAT YOU NEED**

- A floppy magazine (such as a TV guide) that has a page near the middle that features a picture of some pants. The pants should be positioned near the centre of the page. (The pants might be being worn by someone, or may simply be displayed on their own. Plain swimming trunks or bikini bottoms are also acceptable.)
- A pair of pants as identical as possible to the pair in the magazine

• Some sort of container or bag big enough to hide the pants in
• Two identical felt pens, one of which does not work (if necessary just leave one of them with the top off for a few days so that it dries out)

PREPARATION
Use the working felt pen to mark a rough cross on the pants page so that the middle of the cross goes over the pants. This cross should look as if it's been done behind your back without looking. Put the pants in the container and then put it somewhere where it will be in full view of the audience at all times.

PERFORMANCE
Pass the magazine to Betty and explain that you'll want her to draw a big cross on one of the pages. It helps to demonstrate with your finger to show how big the cross should be. Remind her that the cross should not go across two pages. Tell Betty to hold the magazine behind her back and open it somewhere in the middle, then pass her the broken pen. To distract her, tell her to be careful not to get pen marks on her clothes. (Of course, the pen won't be making any marks anyway, but she doesn't know that.) After she's

"made her cross" ask Betty to close up the magazine while it is still behind her back, and pass back the magazine and pen. Look through the magazine for the cross and then produce the pants from the container.

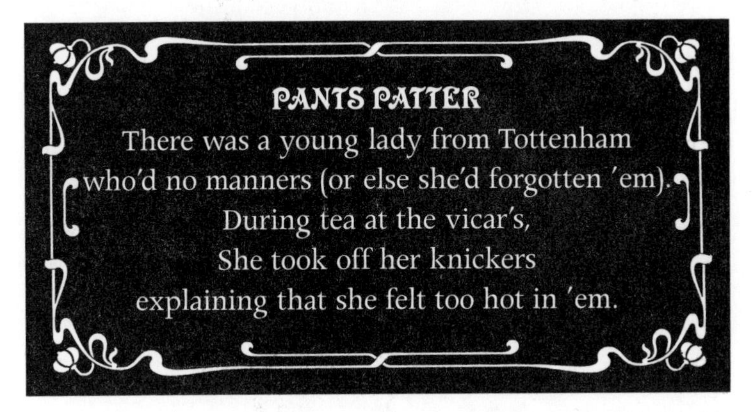


## The Incredible Underwater-trunks Escape ♥♥♥

*A thrilling re-enactment of the death-defying stunt*

Around 100 years ago, the great Houdini terrified audiences by being locked up in a large trunk and dropped into a glass tank of water. A curtain was brought around the tank and everyone waited. Long after everybody thought that he must have drowned,

he would appear dripping wet, exhausted ... but alive. Naturally this trick was dangerous enough, but thanks to the magic of pants we can take it one step further. Instead of using a single trunk, we are going to use a pair of trunks.

The conjuror clasps his hands together and puts them into a pair of swimming trunks. He then invites a volunteer to take the strings of the trunks and tighten them up around his wrists, then tie them with as complicated a knot as possible. Once everything has been secured, the conjuror plunges his bound hands into a bucket of water and one second later...

**PANTSACADABRA!!**

**...the trunks are off and his hands are free. The stunned audience members are allowed to examine the trunks.**

WHAT YOU NEED

- A pair of swimming trunks with a drawstring
- A bit of thin plastic tube about 5 cm long. (If you have an old cheap felt pen, you can chop off the top and bottom and take out the middle bit, leaving you with the tube. If the pen is the same colour as the trunks that's even better.)

- A small nail
- A tiny blob of Blu-tack
- A bucket of water

**PREPARATION**

Turn the trunks inside out. You need to make a small hole in the back of the belt seam and pull through a loop of the drawstring. Feed the loop right through the tube then slip the nail through the end to hold it in place. Squish a tiny blob of Blu-tack into the end of the tube to stop the nail slipping out of the string loop. Turn the trunks back the right way keeping the tube hanging inside the trunks.

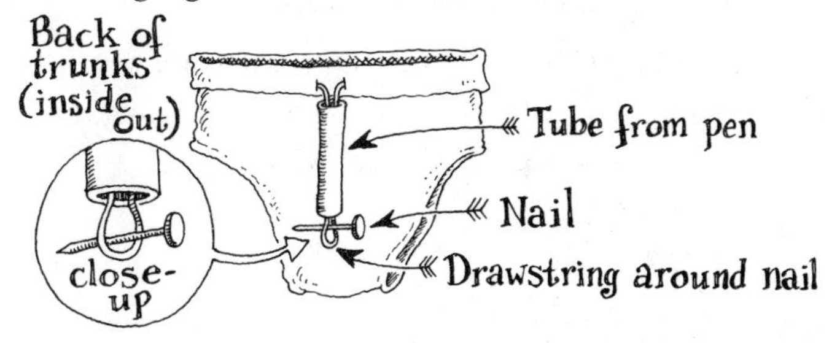


**PERFORMANCE**

Clasp your hands and put the trunks over them – making sure you have the end of the tube between your fingers. Raise your hands up so that the ends of the string are hanging down in front of you, and

invite your volunteer to pull the ends tight and tie them as much as she likes.

For dramatic effect, plunge your hands and the trunks into the bucket of water.

Pull the nail out from the string loop and the trunks will fall free from your hands! If you throw them in the air, everybody will be looking at the trunks, so you can sneakily hold on to the tube and nail and slip them in your pocket when nobody's looking. If the trunks are examined, the knot will still be there, but it's a mystery as to how you got out.

PANTS PATTER

The great 18th-century dandy Beau Legges was so particular about his undergarments that he had his pants specially tailored. The waistbands were made in Paris from the sheerest French elastic, the side twangs were embroidered in Bangkok using Thai silk, the gussets were hand-weaved from Italian lace in Murano and the holes for the leg and convenience openings were taken from a giant Swiss cheese in Zurich.

# The Security Pants ♥♥♥

*The invisible flying £10 note trick*

The conjuror asks for a volunteer who has a £10 note. As he approaches the stage waving the money, the conjuror explains that anyone carrying such a large amount of cash should take special precautions. First of all, it is important to wear some head protection. At this point the conjuror produces a large pair of pants and pulls them on over the volunteer's head.

Next the conjuror says that the £10 note itself should be secured. He produces a pack of envelopes, and takes the £10 note from the volunteer. With a pen,

the conjuror writes the serial number of the £10 note on the top envelope, then puts the £10 note inside. He seals the envelope, passes it to the volunteer for safe keeping and invites him to re-take his seat. But, just as the volunteer is halfway back (and a long distance from the conjuror), the conjuror calls out to him to stop. The conjuror explains that he wants to check that the Security Pants are working. He asks a second volunteer to be a robber. The robber takes the envelope from the first volunteer and hurries away to a back corner of the stage.

The robber is then asked to open the envelope and take out the £10 note but...

## PANTSACADABRA!!

THE £10 HAS DISAPPEARED! THERE'S JUST THIS NOTE...

The £10 note has been transferred to the security pants for safe keeping

The conjuror asks the first volunteer to reach up to the Security Pants on his head and insert his fingers into the convenience hole. What does he find?

## PANTSACADABRA AGAIN!!

## WHAT YOU NEED

- A large pair of pants with a convenience hole
- A pack of envelopes with the wrapping band round it. The envelopes must be the sort that open at the end rather than along the top.
- A reasonably new £10 note
- A piece of paper the same size as a £10 note
- A pen

## PREPARATION

The pack of envelopes should all have their flaps sticking up. With the backs of the envelopes facing you, remove the top envelope. Write the serial number of your £10 note neatly across the back of the next envelope in the pack, just under where the wrapping band lies. Take a piece of paper the same size as a £10 note and write on it: "The £10 note has been transferred to the Security Pants for safe keeping." Put this paper into the envelope on which you've just written the serial number. With a light

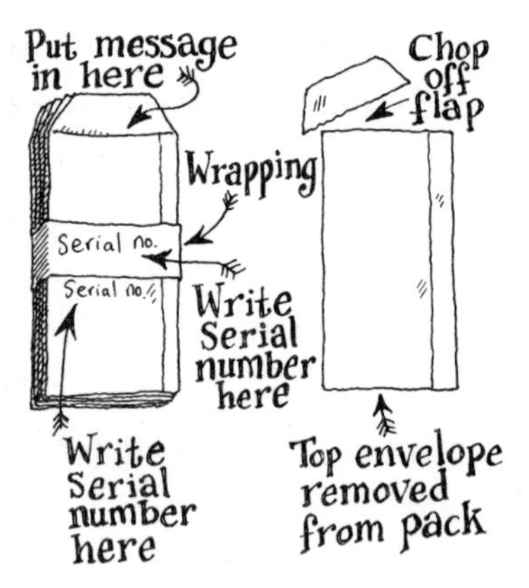

pencil, write the same serial number very faintly across the wrapping band of the envelopes.

Now take the envelope you removed, cut off the flap very neatly and then slide it back into the wrapping on top of the pack.

Turn the pants inside out and sew up the inside of the convenience hole. When the pants are turned right way out again, the convenience hole will in effect have become a small pocket. Fold up your £10 note very tightly and tuck it into the convenience hole. The £10 note should be completely hidden until such time as it is required. (If necessary, secure the note with a small paper clip.)

When you come to perform, ensure that you have the same pen that you used to write the number on the envelope.

NOTE: You may wish to wear the pants before the trick and remove them when required. If you do so, remember that the convenience hole is sewn up, so do not attempt to use it for the conventional purpose.

## PERFORMANCE

Select a volunteer with a £10 note. If possible, ask volunteers to hold their £10 notes up, and pick a person with a £10 note that looks in a similar state to yours, i.e. reasonably new.

When your volunteer steps up with his £10 note, put the security pants straight on to his head, taking care that he is not aware of the hidden £10 note.

Take the offered £10 note and explain that you're going to record its number for safe keeping. Hold the note on top of the pack of envelopes and pretend you're writing the serial number of the note on to the top envelope. In reality, you copy the serial number that you wrote faintly on the wrapping. (Do this quite quickly, and say the numbers as you write them down. This makes the switch look more convincing.)

Slide the £10 note down into the top envelope. Make sure nobody sees that the flap is missing.

Here comes the clever move that's worth practising: take hold of the top flap on the pack of envelopes. When you pull it out, you are secretly leaving the top envelope where it is and instead you're taking the envelope with the message inside it. As you pull the envelope out, let the wrapping slide a small distance down the pack to cover up the serial number on the top envelope.

Seal up the envelope, pass it to your volunteer, and the trick is done. You can even suggest that your volunteer holds the envelope up to the light – he'll see the shadow of what looks like the £10 note inside it. All that's left to do is let him walk well away from you, then get your "robber" to take the envelope from him. (As she does so, casually discard the other envelopes somewhere.) Make sure the robber has moved well back from both of you before she opens the envelope, and then the volunteer finds the £10 note in the pants.

NOTE: at the end of the show, make sure you don't lose the pack of envelopes. Otherwise, this trick will cost you £10. And make sure you get your pants back, too.

# Avoiding a Pantastrophe

*For those days when you feel like you've just reached the last sheet on the roll...*

...Suddenly the last sheet comes off and it becomes clear that the rest of the toilet roll just has false ends. The centre section is hollow. A shower of confetti falls out revealing the naked cardboard tube in the middle.

WHAT YOU NEED

- A new toilet roll
- An empty toilet roll
- Confetti
- A long stiff sheet of paper the same width and colour as a piece of the toilet paper and about five times as long. (You'll probably need to tape a few sheets together to make it long enough.)
- A pair of black or dark-coloured pants (not too big or heavy)
- A "magic wand". (You can either make a black stick with white ends, or any old stick will do.)

PREPARATION

You need to make a gimmick* out of the empty roll in exactly the same way as described in *The Burrowed Pants* on page 89. When you've made your narrowed tube, take the pants and jam them tightly inside it so that they don't fall out.

Take the full toilet roll, and tear off a strip of about five sheets. Unroll the next few sheets, put glue along the edges (but don't let it go over the edges) then glue them down again. With a sharp art knife

* Deceiver's definition: GIMMICK – if you don't know what a gimmick is by now, then tough luck.

(be careful!) cut into the roll all the way round about 2 cm in from each end. You should then be able to remove all the middle section of the toilet paper leaving the ends on. Apply more glue to the insides of these ends to hold the thin rolls of paper together and make them more solid.

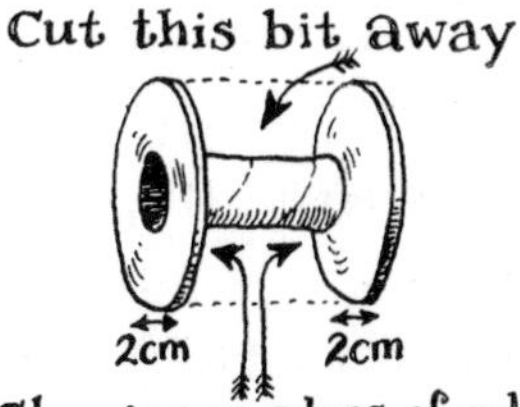


Glue the five sheets you tore off earlier to the end of the stiff sheet of paper. Lie this long strip on a table, then put a handful of confetti on the stiff sheet of paper. Put the prepared toilet roll on the sheet of paper and roll it up so that the stiff sheet of paper goes round first, trapping the confetti, followed by the sheets of normal toilet paper, as shown.

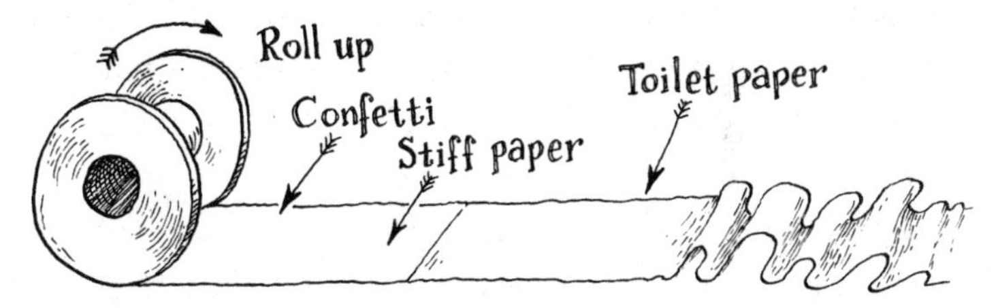


When finished the toilet roll should look quite normal, but be careful not to squeeze it.

Before the performance, you need to hide the gimmick. If you are wearing a coat (or jacket or

cardigan), use a paper clip to fix the gimmick to your belt under the coat flap. If you can paint the gimmick the same colour as your trousers or skirt, so much the better. Otherwise, you can Blu-tack the gimmick to the edge of the table away from the audience.

**PERFORMANCE**

Display the toilet roll in your left hand, and with your right hand put your wand through the hole. When you spin the roll on the wand, be careful not to push down on the centre of the roll and squash it, and spin it so that the paper does NOT unwind.

With your left hand, take the roll of paper from the wand, hold it up and look at it. As you do so, put the wand on the table with your right hand and then slip your hand below the table and secretly grab the gimmick in your right hand. Make sure the narrow end of the gimmick is uppermost. Here comes the clever move...

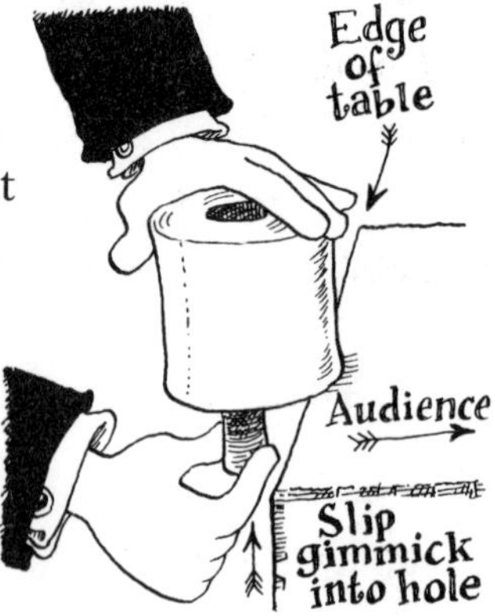

Bring your left hand down and put the edge of the roll on the very back edge of the table. As you do so, bring the gimmick up with your right hand and slip it inside the roll. Then push the roll on to the table with your right hand as if just making sure it wasn't going to fall off.

This should all be done in one smooth movement in under a second – try not to look at the roll as you are doing it.

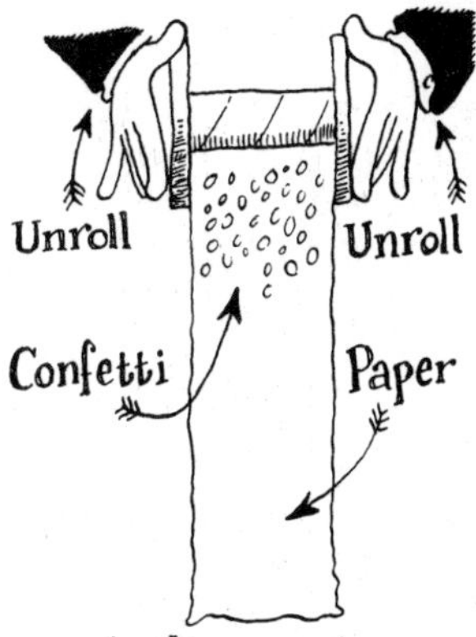


Mention that the roll has been sabotaged, then pick up the roll without letting the audience see directly into either end. Hold the roll sideways on to the audience between both hands with the loose flap of paper hanging down towards you. Slowly unroll the paper until it falls away and the confetti falls out. (Some people will think this is the end of the trick, so you're really going to surprise them.)

When the laughter has subsided, hold the edge of the roll with your left hand and (keeping your finger just over the edge of the hole to stop the gimmick coming out) take the wand and push it into the other end. The pants will fall out.

Once again you can spin the roll on the wand to show there is "nothing" inside the roll.

NOTES: Although the pants should be of a dark colour so that they will not be obvious if the end of the roll is glimpsed while they are in place, it might be amusing to decorate them with the words "Emergency Pants".
When first showing the toilet roll, don't mention the hole too much because the audience will start to get suspicious as to what will happen. In other words, don't say, "Look at the hole, see how empty it is, there is nothing in there is there?" As soon as you do that, they'll be trying to spot when you put something in it. By putting the wand through the hole and letting the roll spin, and then having a quick look at them down the hole, the audience will know it's empty but won't be alerted as to what you're about to do.

# Escape from Pantsatraz

Many devilish tails are told of Pantsatraz Prison. Built on a rock island in a sea of sharks, countless scores of prisoners have met gruesome deaths in their futile attempts to escape. Those that were recaptured were tightly secured to prevent any further attempts to leave. These offenders were not only bound hand and foot, but were further secured by four sets of reinforced manacle pants and then bundled into a sack. This illusion not only conjures up all the grim horrors of Pantsatraz, but allows you to effect a seemingly impossible escape!

A volunteer is invited to step up from the audience, then helps with putting the conjuror's arms and legs through the holes of four pairs of strong pants as shown in the picture.

Next the volunteer takes a piece of rope and ties it around one of the conjuror's wrists and then the other. Finally, the volunteer ties a second piece of rope around the conjuror's ankles in the same way and then puts him into a large duvet cover.

Within just a few short hours the conjuror emerges from the duvet cover with his hands and ankles still tied, but...

**PANTSACADABRA!!**

**...he has escaped from all four pairs of pants.**

WHAT YOU NEED

- Four pairs of big strong pants
- Two pieces of rope
- A large duvet cover (preferably light-coloured then it's easier to see what you're doing when you're inside)

PERFORMANCE

Get the volunteer to help put the pants on you and tie the ropes as shown on the previous page. The ropes should be tied in the same way as described in *The Knicker Nicker.* To remove the pants linking your left arm and left leg, you use *The Side-twang Release...*

## The Pant Practioner's Guide to...
# THE SIDE-TWANG RELEASE

*This is similar to* The Gusset Release *on page 100 but needs to be done in two stages.*

*Push the side twang of the pants along the edge of your wrist inside the rope loop, then bring it round over your fingers.*

*The side twang can then be brought back along the other side of your wrist and out through the loop.*

*Tuck the loose side of the pants through the rope loop round your ankle – then you can pull the entire pair of pants right off.*

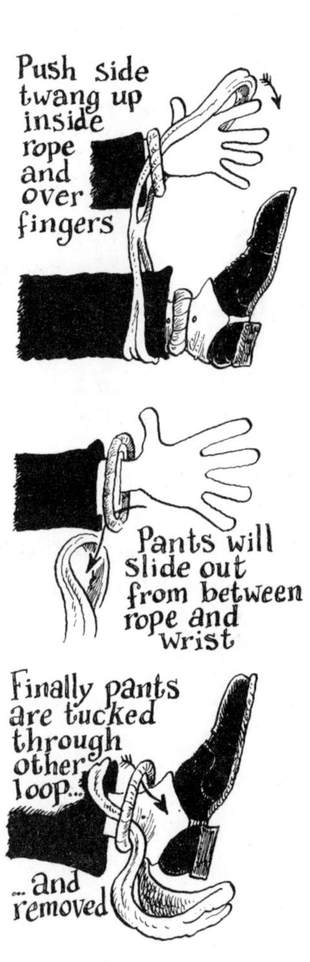

*Using* **The Side-twang Release,** ***you can remove both pairs of pants that link your arms and legs. You can also use*** **The Side-twang Release** ***to remove the pants from your wrists and ankles, but if the pants are loose and slinky enough, you may prefer the gusset release.***

**HISTORICAL NOTE**

*This trick is a modern adaptation of the Great Gusset's original Prison Island Escape. When he first performed at the Grand Thong Palace, he rather cunningly created the illusion of a bleak prison island by tipping a sack of stones into the middle of the Empress's nephew's paddling pool and sitting on them. To his dismay the Empress decided to enhance the illusion by putting some piranha fish in the water to represent the sharks circling the island. Although he managed to escape the pants with ease, the Great Gusset was unable to get off his island until one of the fish accidentally bit into the side of the pool and the water all drained away. It was then but a simple matter for the Great Gusset to gather up the gasping fish in the pants and pass them around to the delighted audience to use as nut crackers.*

# The Drink Dispantser

*When you're panting for a drink...*

Halfway through his performance, the conjuror says that he is starting to feel exhausted and needs a refreshing drink.

He holds up a large pair of bright orange pants and explains that these are no ordinary pants – in fact, this is a drink dispantser. He shows the pants front and back and even turns them inside out to prove that they are empty, then inserts a coin into the convenience hole. He then reaches inside them and...

**PANTSACADABRA!!**

**...he pulls out a real glass of orange juice. He takes a drink and then offers it to members of the audience.**

**WHAT YOU NEED**

- A pair of very large pants, preferably of a bright colour
- A small slim glass tumbler
- A strong elastic band
- A small piece of material the same colour as your jacket (preferably both should be dark coloured or black)
- A small piece of polythene – a piece of a plastic carrier bag is fine
- A suitable drink in the glass

**PREPARATION**

Fill your glass with any non-fizzy drink. If the colour of the drink matches the pants it adds to the effect. Put a piece of polythene over the top of the glass, and then over the polythene put the piece of material that matches your jacket. Fold these both down the sides of the glass, then secure them tightly using the elastic band.

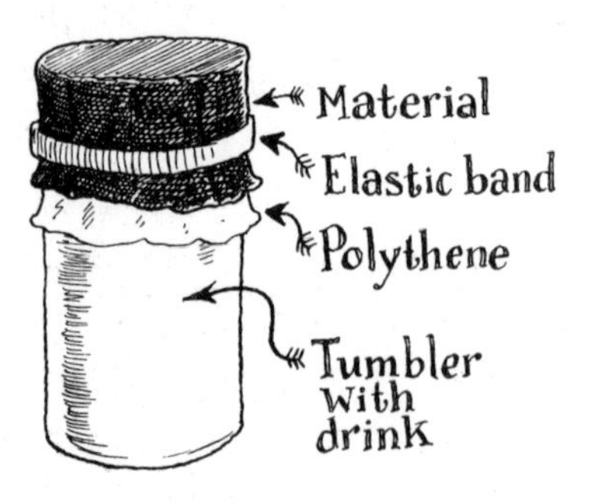

Tip the glass upside down to ensure no liquid comes out. Put the prepared glass and the pants together somewhere out of sight but within easy reach for the performance.

**PERFORMANCE**

Immediately before the trick, you must secretly put the loaded glass under the top of your left arm with the cloth top facing towards the audience. If you briefly turn your right side towards the audience and bend over slightly, as if looking for the pants, the glass may be quickly grabbed and positioned with the right hand while the pants are being found. You will find you can still move the lower part of your left arm quite a lot while keeping a grip on the glass. Because the top matches your jacket, it will be almost invisible to the audience.

Grab the pants in both hands and then holding them apart by the side twangs, turn to face the audience. Reverse your hands to show the pants front and back. You may even turn them inside out. If you keep the pants moving and held quite high, the audience will not notice the hidden glass.

Finally hold your left forearm across in front of your chest, and pass your right hand in front, then drape the pants over your left arm. Let go with your right hand leaving the pants hanging down from your arm directly in front of the glass.

If the pants have a convenience hole, a coin may be inserted with your right hand at this point.

With your right hand, reach behind the pants and bring the glass forward, turning it the right way up. As you do this, bring the pants back so that they drape over the glass. Ease the elastic band off the glass with your right thumb, so allowing the cover to come away.

With your left hand, grab the pants and the loose cover of the glass and pull them away leaving your right hand holding the glass. As everyone admires the

glass, let the cover and elastic band fall from the pants out of sight.

NOTE: This trick may be done using a large pair of pants borrowed from a member of the audience. If you are planning to use borrowed pants, put milk in the glass, because white is the normal colour for most pairs of surgical pants.

# A Sock in the Pants

*An unwelcome visitor in the drawers drawer*

The conjuror then invites a volunteer to come on stage and lend him his pants. The conjuror produces a pair of his own pants, an old sock and a box.

*"Imagine that our pants were to share the same drawer, which already had an old sock in it."*

So saying, the conjuror drops the sock into the box. He continues: *"Here's my new system to ensure that our pants can't get mixed up with the sock."*

The conjuror takes the two pairs of pants and fixes them together with a safety pin, then drops them into the box.

*"Now there's no way that the sock can interfere with our pants. Let's just check."*

The conjuror reaches into the box and pulls out the two pairs of pants...

**PANTSACADABRA!!**

**...pinned between the two pairs of pants is the old sock.**

The conjuror tips the box upside-down to show it is empty.

**WHAT YOU NEED**

- A pair of double-bottom pants (see page 54)
- A pair of old thin socks
- Two safety pins

- Two old cereal boxes the same size (one box should have the lid flaps still attached)
- Sticky tape

**PREPARATION**

First you need to make a trick box with a secret panel. Take one of the cereal boxes and remove the lid flaps at the back and sides, just leaving the lid flap at the front.

To make the secret panel, take the other cereal box and cut out the whole of the front side. Slide this panel into the first box behind the front panel, making sure that the blank side faces inwards. Trim the panel so that it fits exactly inside the box and goes right to the edges. Using a strip of tape, stick the panel along the bottom edge (see below). With the panel pushed against the front of the box and the lid flap folded inwards, when you look inside the box the secret panel should be invisible.

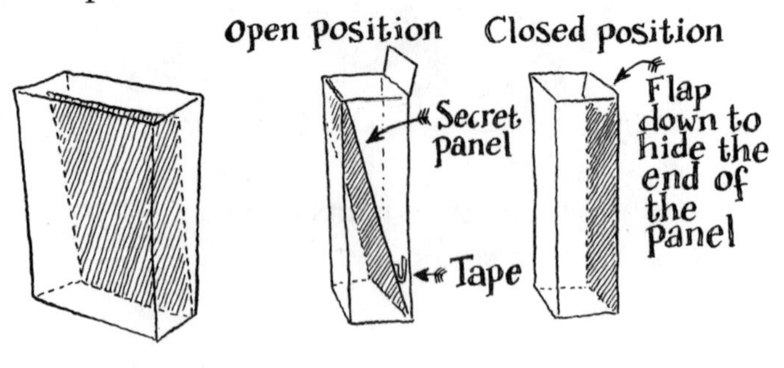

Next, you need to organize your socks. If possible, the socks should be the same colour as the double-bottom pants. If they are not the same colour, you need to get a bit of material the same colour as the pants and sew a trim around the top edge of each sock (see above).

Take one of the socks and, using a safety pin, pin the end of the toe under the label of your double-bottom pants. Now, push the rest of the sock down into the pocket of the pants, just leaving the very last edge of the sock sticking out. This edge should be the same colour as the pants and so will not be noticed. Smooth the label down over the safety pin to hide it.

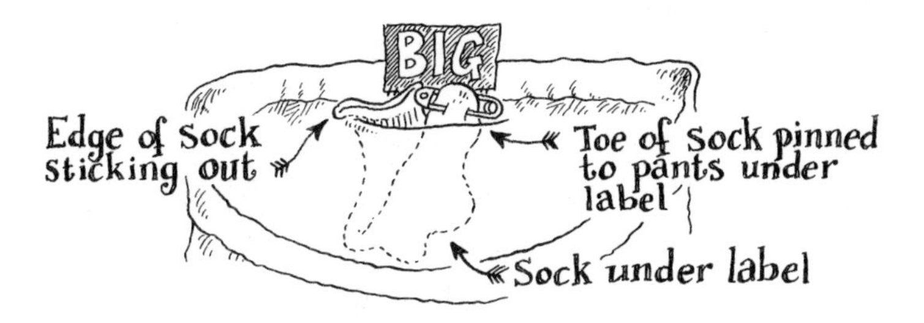

## PERFORMANCE

When Mr Pexton arrives on stage, ask him to hold on to his pants as you show the (other) sock. Take the box and secretly open the secret panel. Drop the sock in and then close the panel and fold the lid flap down over it. Put the box to one side and take Mr Pexton's pants and your own. Using the other safety pin, make it look as if you are fixing the back of his pants to the back of your own pants. In reality you pin his pants to the edge of the sock sticking out of your double-bottom pants. If you hold on to your pants keeping a grip on the hidden sock, you can swing Mr Pexton's pants around to show they are properly connected. Drop the two pairs of pants inside the box.

When pulling the pants from the box, hold the box with your left hand, keeping your fingers across the top. Pull Mr Pexton's pants first through a gap in your fingers, but then, as your pants reach your fingers, stop them coming out until the pinned sock has been pulled from the pocket.

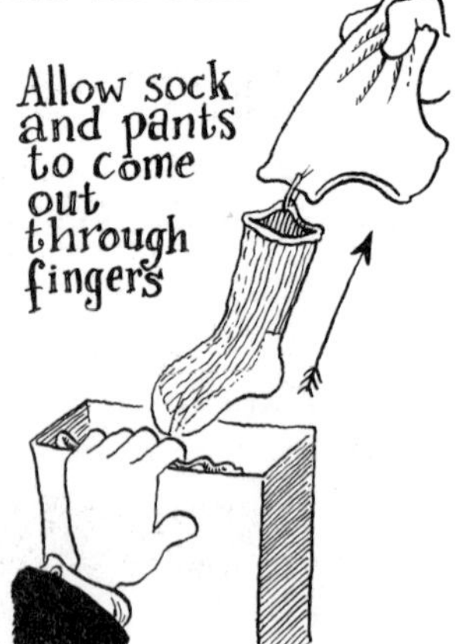

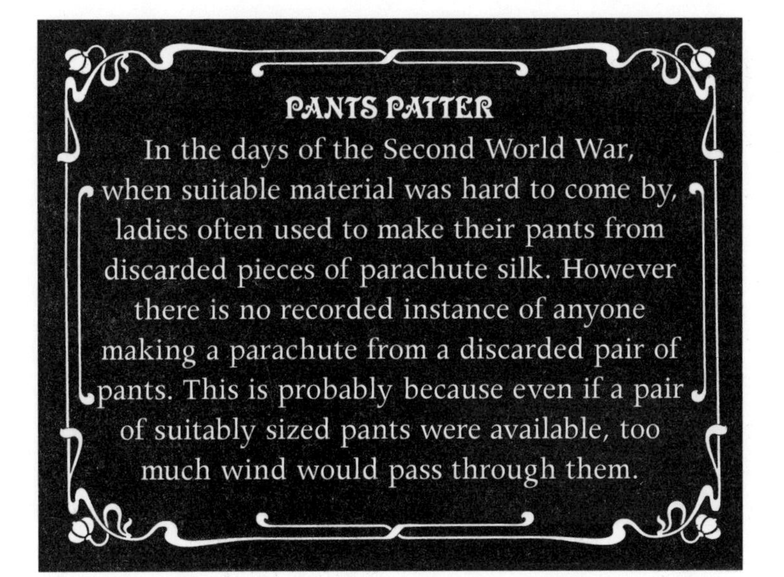

**PANTS PATTER**

In the days of the Second World War, when suitable material was hard to come by, ladies often used to make their pants from discarded pieces of parachute silk. However there is no recorded instance of anyone making a parachute from a discarded pair of pants. This is probably because even if a pair of suitably sized pants were available, too much wind would pass through them.

## The Ghost's Pants

*A classic escape*

I NEED A VOLUNTEER TO BE THE GHOST.
WHOOO!
I PUT THE ROPES AROUND YOU SO THAT EACH HAND HAS A LONG END AND A SHORT END.
WE HOLD THE ROPE ACROSS THE FRONT WITH ONE PAIR OF GHOST PANTS...
...AND THE SECOND PAIR OF GHOST PANTS GOES AROUND THE BACK.
NOW I NEED TWO STRONG ASSISTANTS FROM THE AUDIENCE. EACH OF YOU TAKE A SHORT ROPE...

... AND FINALLY I CROSS OVER THE LONG ROPES AND PASS THEM TO MY ASSISTANTS.
IF THE ROPES ARE PULLED HARD THEN THE PERSON IN THE MIDDLE WILL BE SQUASHED TO AN AGONIZING DEATH. UNLESS, OF COURSE, HE'S A...
PANTSACADABRA!!
...GHOST!

WHAT YOU NEED

- Two identical strong ropes each about 2½ m long
- Two very large pairs of pants – preferably in different bright colours
- A small piece of cotton the same colour as the ropes

PREPARATION

Lie the two ropes alongside each other and then, about 1 m from the end, tie them together with the white cotton. When you hold the ropes, put your hand around where the cotton is and let the ends dangle freely so that nobody is aware that they are joined together.

PERFORMANCE

Invite your ghost on stage. With one hand over the cotton tie, grab the ropes towards the far end and pull on them to show they are strong.

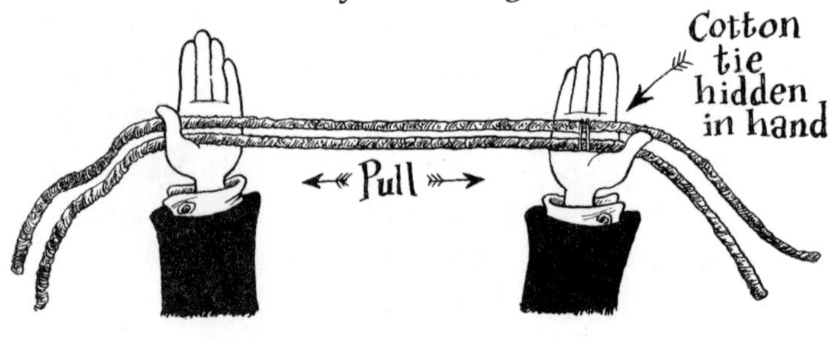

Ask the ghost to face the audience. Then explain that you need him to hold the ends of both ropes, but first you have to put them round his neck. Also tell him that the ends need to be uneven.

Walk around the back of the ghost and, as you do so, quickly swap the ends of the rope over as shown in the diagram.

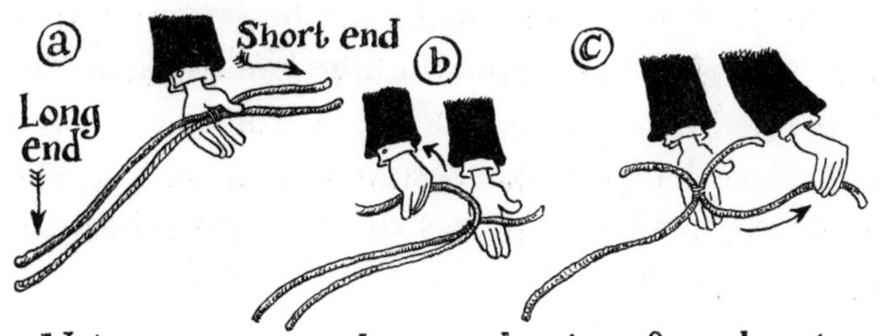


Note: ropes are shown shorter for clarity

Ask your ghost to hold his arms straight out in front of him. Hold the section of ropes with the cotton tie directly behind the ghost's neck with one hand and keep it there while you arrange the rest of the rope ends with your other hand. You need to drape the ropes around his shoulders and pass them along his arms so he can take the ends in his hands. He should finish up with one long end and one short end in each hand. Make sure the ropes aren't too tight, let go of the cotton tie. It should end up like this:

Put the first pair of pants on his arms from the front, and pull them up so the side twangs go over his shoulders. This will hold the ropes around his back in place. Then let him move his arms down (still holding the ropes) and help him get the second pair of pants on from the back, as if helping him into a small waistcoat. When both pairs of pants are on he can lower his arms and release the ropes.

Invite your two assistants from the audience to stand either side of the ghost. Pass the shorter rope in each hand to the nearest assistant, then take the longer ropes and cross them over with a twist. Pass the ends to the assistants. When they pull the ropes, the cotton will snap and the ropes will come free of the pants.

A true miracle.

NOTE: The two pairs of pants may be borrowed from your assistants. However, if bringing your assistants to the stage before the pants are in place, make sure that they stand forward of your volunteer, so that they do not see the cotton tie holding the ropes behind him.

# The Extraordinary Switching Pants

*Was he really wearing her knickers?*

The conjuror borrows a pair of pants from a gentleman in the audience and puts them on over his own trousers. He then invites a lady to join him on stage and requests her to display the pants she is wearing. Once both pairs of pants have been viewed to the satisfaction of the audience, the conjuror steps behind a screen, removes the borrowed pants and places them in a white bag. He then returns on stage holding the bag and places it somewhere in clear view.

The conjuror then invites the lady to step behind the screen to remove her pants and goes to help her place them in a black plastic bag. The lady returns to the stage holding the bag. At no point does she go anywhere near the white bag.

The conjuror takes the white bag, then reaches for his wand – it transpires that he has left his wand behind the screen, so he quickly gets it and returns to the stage. He waves his wand and then both he and the lady open their bags...

**PANTSACADABRA!!**

**...the conjuror has the lady's pants in his white bag, and the lady has the pants borrowed from the gentleman in her black bag. The pants are returned to the correct owners.**

WHAT YOU NEED

- A screen large enough for people to hide behind
- A few hooks at the back suitable for hanging bags on
- Two pairs of matching carrier bags. (For the purposes of this explanation we'll say that you have two white bags and two black bags.)
- A spare pair of medium-sized pants
- A magic wand of any description

PREPARATION

Put the screen to the back of the stage. Hanging on hooks behind the screen is one of the black bags and

also one of the white bags with the spare pair of pants in it. Have the two other bags in your pockets and hold the magic wand.

**PERFORMANCE**

This is a truly astonishing illusion, and well worth some careful practise. Follow the instructions carefully using the key below and you can't go wrong.

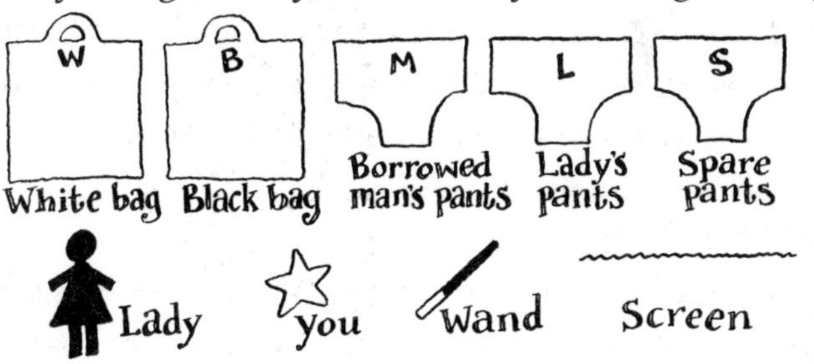


Show the audience the two empty bags you are holding – one white and one black. You should also be holding your magic wand.

Borrow a pair of pants from a man in the audience and put them on over your trousers. Next, invite a lady from the audience to come on stage and display her pants. Pass her the black bag you are holding.

Next, you explain that you are going to remove the borrowed pants and put them in the white bag. But, as there is a lady on stage, for modesty's sake you'll pop behind the screen.

Behind the screen, hang up the white bag you had with you on one of the hooks. Stick your wand somewhere behind the screen where you can easily get it later. You then take off the borrowed pants and put them in the spare black bag, which is also on a hook. Step back on stage with the other white bag that contains the spare pants (but everyone will assume it's the borrowed pants). Put this white bag to one side, where everyone can see it.

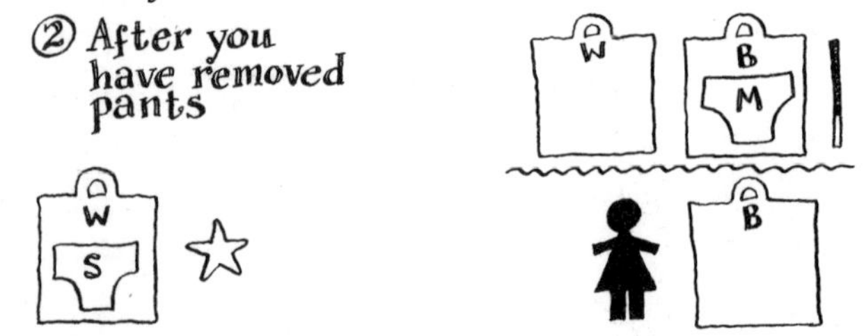


Invite the lady behind the screen, take the black bag from her and hang it up. Make sure you're

standing between her and the hooks, then ask her to remove her pants and pass them to you. Allow her to adjust her outfit and step out from behind the screen. In the few seconds that she is thus occupied, turn to the hooks and quickly slip her pants into the white bag on the hook. Then take the black bag containing the borrowed pants, step out from behind the screen and pass the black bag to her.

The audience will assume that the black bag contains her pants.

The lady stands well away from the white bag you placed on stage earlier.

Hold up the white bag, pretend you are about to do the magic, but have lost your wand. Dash behind the screen, and as you are getting your wand, very quickly swap the white bags over.

Step on stage again, wave your wand and ask the lady to open her bag as you open yours. The "miracle" has happened.

NOTES: If you don't want your lady volunteer to suspect how the trick works, be careful not to let her see which bag you put her pants into. However, if you have a friend whom you can trust with the secret, you could plan beforehand that she goes behind the screen alone, puts her pants into the white bag and brings out the black bag with the borrowed pants in it. Even if people suspect that she is a plant*, they will be mystified as to how the pants were swapped over.

If for any reason it is not suitable for people to swap their pants, this trick can work equally well by getting people to swap their vests or a shoe in exactly the same manner.

*Deceiver's definition: PLANT – a secret assistant pretending to be a normal member of the audience.

# Designer Tricks

*These are theatre tricks requiring more elaborate props. Not everyone will have the skill, time and patience required to create the items needed for these tricks, but if the inside of your wardrobe is wallpapered, then this is the section for you...*

# Pants in a Can

*How to keep your frillies fresh*

PANTSACADABRA!!

WHAT YOU NEED

- An empty, and clean, normal-sized soup or beans tin with the lid removed (make sure it has no sharp edges)
- A large sheet of card that's black on one side and white on the other (you can get this from a stationer's or an art shop)
- A bright pair of pants that will fit inside the tin
- Tape, black paint, other paints, stickers, scissors

PREPARATION

Cut two rectangles out of the cardboard measuring 34 cm x 14 cm and 42 cm x 14 cm. In the bigger piece cut a hole measuring 4 cm x 4 cm.

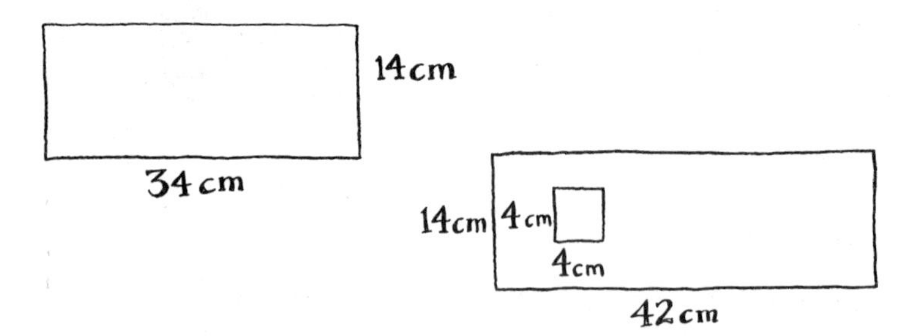


Use paints and stickers to decorate the white sides of the two pieces of card, making them look as different as possible. Then roll them into tubes with the black side on the inside and stick them with tape.

Cut out two pieces of the card, each big enough to go halfway round the tin. (They should each measure about 11 cm x 12 cm.) Write "BOTTOM" in big fancy letters on the white side of one piece of card and stick it on the front of the tin so the letters can be seen. Stick the other piece of card on the back side of the tin but with the black side showing. Take care not to make any marks on this black side.

Put your pants in the tin and put the tin on the table with the black side facing the audience. Put the smaller tube over the tin, and then put the bigger tube over the smaller tube with the hole facing the audience. You're ready.

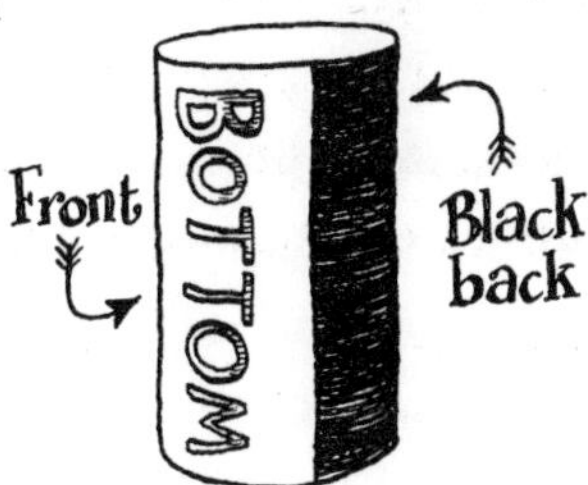


**PERFORMANCE**

Start by showing the "two" tubes, one inside the other. The audience don't know about the tin yet. Lift up the outer tube and show that it is empty. Replace it and lift up the second tube. The audience will not see the tin because the black side will not show against the black inside of the outer tube.

Replace the second tube, then reach in for the tin. Before pulling it out, turn the tin round so that the lettered side faces the audience. Pull it out and remove your pants.

## Fancy Pants ♥♥

*A new forcing trick with a dazzling conclusion*

The conjuror calls a volunteer from the audience and produces a special pack of cards – each card has a different pair of pants pictured on it – he asks the volunteer to choose a pair that would suit him. The cards are dealt face down on to a table.

**WHAT YOU NEED**

- A pair of fancy pants to wear
- A special pack of pants cards (see below)

**THE PACK OF PANTS CARDS**

This is a special pack of at least 20 cards, on which all the backs are the same. On the fronts of five of the cards there are pictures of different pants, but all the other cards show the same pair of fancy pants. There are different ways you can make the pack. You can either get an old pack of playing cards (it doesn't have to be a full set) and stick white stickers over the face of each card, or you can get a neat box of plain white cards from a stationery shop.

You might like to design your own pants for this trick. Otherwise, you can use the following pictures which you can trace, photocopy or scan with a computer. You will also need to make yourself a real pair of pants to match the fancy pants on the cards.

**PREPARATION**

Put your fancy pants on under your dress or trousers and arrange the cards like this:

**PERFORMANCE**

Choose a volunteer and hold the pack of cards face down in your hand. Turn over the top card and lay it face up on the table. Ask your volunteer if she thinks these pants would suit you. Turn over the next three cards one by one and ask if either of these would be better.

Once you have laid the top four cards face up on the table, turn them over and push them into a little pile. Explain that none of those pants are fancy enough for you, so you'll try to find a fancier pair. Start to deal the cards from the deck face down on to the pile, and ask the volunteer to stop you at any point. As soon as she says stop, you turn over the last card you dealt. (This will be one of the fancy pants cards.) Then you say, "Shall we see if these pants suit me?" and reveal your pants.

NOTE: If your volunteer doesn't say stop until the last card, turn it over anyway and say, "You're too late and, besides, I don't like these pants." You then leave the last card on the table, pick up the face-down pack and again deal the cards face down to the table one by one, but insist that she makes her mind up quickly this time. (You don't want to have to stop on one of the last four cards.)

# The Sugar Plum Fairy's Pants Dance

*You've seen the ballet, now admire the bloomers*

The conjuror asks who has heard of *"The Dance Of The Sugar Plum Fairy"*. He then explains that sadly the fairy is no longer with us, but luckily he does have a pair of her pants, which he is wearing. However, as they are magic fairy pants, occasionally they like to escape his trousers and do a little pants dance on their own. He picks up a large piece of silk and holds it across in front of him so that the upper part of his trousers and chest are hidden from the audience. He then announces that the pants are indeed coming out to dance. There are a few ripples and bulges in the cloth and then...

**PANTSACADABRA!!**

**...the little lacy pants appear at the top of the cloth and proceed to skip and pirouette around on their own.**

## WHAT YOU NEED

- A silk cloth about 75 cm square
- A thin stick the same length as one side of the cloth
- A false rubber hand (we'll assume the rubber hand is on the right in these instructions). You can get rubber hands from most trick shops, but try to get one that looks like your real hand, not a monster or werewolf hand, unless of course you happen to be a monster or a werewolf.
- A little pair of lacy panties
- 60 cm of stiff wire (a thin coat hanger is ideal)

## PREPARATION

Glue the stick along one edge of the cloth, with the cloth wrapped around it so the stick does not show. Fix the fingers of the rubber hand to one end of the stick as if they are holding it. When you grab the other end of the stick and hold it so that the cloth hangs across your chest, to the audience it should look like you are holding it with two hands.

Put one end of the wire up through one of the legholes of the pants, and fix this end right along the front of the waistband. Where the wire comes out of the leghole, bend it backwards. Put a few bends in the long end to make it easier to hold.

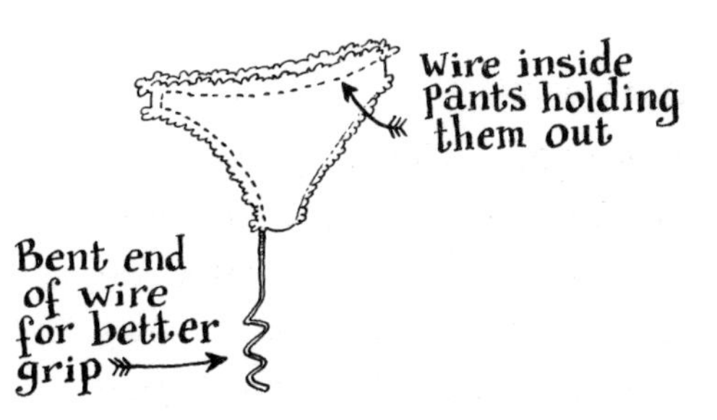


Before the performance, tuck the wire of the pants down the back of your trousers and hide the pants under your jacket. Lay the stick on the table with the cloth bundled over it (not wrapped around). When you quickly pick up the stick with your left hand and raise it to chest height, the cloth should fall away revealing the dummy right hand.

**PERFORMANCE**

Reach for the stick with both hands, but grab it with your left hand and quickly raise it to your chest. The cloth should fall down revealing the dummy right hand, and hiding the fact that your right hand and arm are free. Make sure that you are facing the audience and that no one can see round the sides of the cloth. Reach your right hand behind you and grab the wire holding the pants.

At first just brush the pants against the back of the cloth so that it creates some mysterious bulges,

then let the very edge of the pants appear over the top. Before doing a full pants dance, bring the pants back down behind the cloth and have them appear out to the side of the cloth or from the bottom.

Once you're ready to dance, you can wiggle and twiddle the wire for comic effect, but make sure the bottom of the pants never goes higher than the stick or the wire will become obvious.

At the end of the trick, bundle the pants and wire up in the cloth and put to the side.

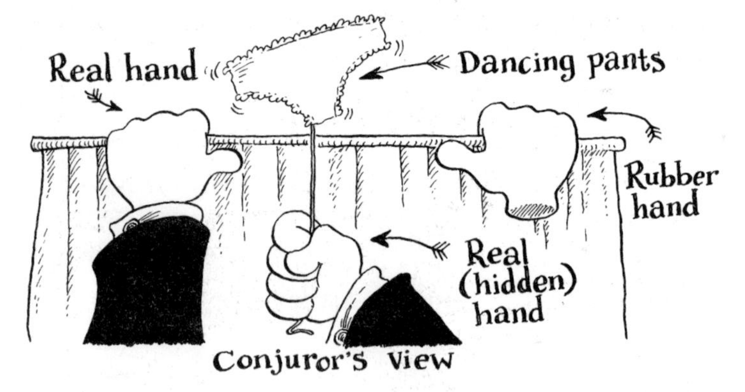


NOTE: To add to the illusion of the pants coming alive, before the pants actually appear pull some strange, contorted faces. This will give the impression that the pants really are struggling to escape from your trousers all on their own.

# The Phenomenal Floating Frillies

*A truly astonishing levitation* of lingerie*

The conjuror has a cabinet on the table beside him. Through a large hole in the front, a rope is seen hanging across the inside of the cabinet like a washing line. The conjuror borrows a pair of pants, then steps behind the box. Reaching in from the top he pegs the pants on to the washing line. He then unhooks the two ends of the washing line from the sides of the box and lets them fall loose but...

**PANTSACADABRA!!**

**...the pants stay where they are in mid-air!**

*Deceiver's definition: LEVITATION – where an object or person appears to hover in the air with no means of support.

The conjuror then takes a solid metal hoop and passes it over and around the pants to show that they are not suspended by invisible threads or any other hidden apparatus. Finally the ends of the washing line are reconnected, the pants are unpegged and returned unharmed to the owner who may pass them round so that everyone can see that the pants have not been interfered with in any way.

## HOW TO BUILD YOUR OWN PANTS-LEVITATION CABINET

Please note that this trick is a real showpiece and will fully reward the time required in the preparation. Thankfully, modern developments in magic now make it possible to build your own cabinet reasonably quickly, but as you do so, spare a thought for the Great Gusset. When he first devised the trick, he spent many long hours building a solid wooden cabinet complete with brass fittings and leather trimmings. As later magicians worked on improving his design, they invented the cardboard box and the wire coat hanger – items that have since found other uses in the retail, packing and dry-cleaning industries. This is a perfect example of the beneficial effect magic has had on mankind.

## WHAT YOU NEED

- A big strong cardboard box measuring at least 60 cm x 60 cm x 60 cm
- A piece of thickish rope (a section of one of those brightly coloured thick skipping ropes is ideal)
- Some strong stiff wire, e.g. a wire coat hanger
- Matt black paint, stickers, scissors, strong tape, silver tape, glue
- Two small keyrings (available from Pexton's Hardware Supplies)
- Two clothes pegs – the kind with a spring are best

## PREPARATION

Cut a hole in the front of the box that goes almost to the edges. The box should have four flaps that make the lid. Remove the two flaps at the sides and the back one, just leaving the lid flap joined to the front of the

box. Use the tape to stick the front flap down securely to the sides of the box, so making it sturdier. This should leave half of the top open for you to get your hands down inside during the performance.

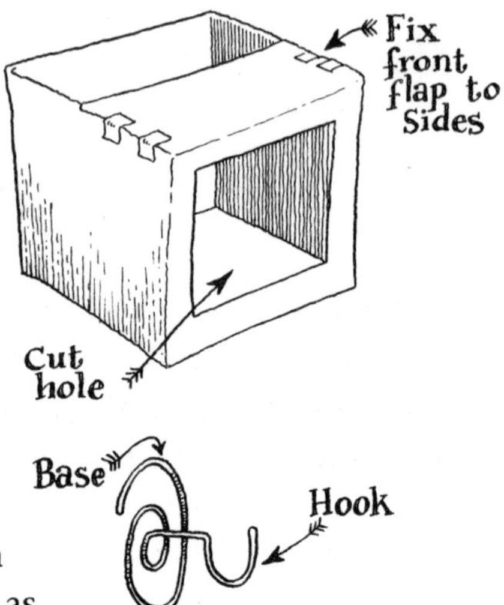


Cut two bits of wire, each about 15 cm long. Bend them into a hook shape with a base as shown in the diagram.

Using the end of the wire, make two small holes – one in each side of the box. The holes should be almost to the back of the box and near the top. Put a hook through each hole and then use the tape to fix the base of each hook securely in place on the outside. Paint the box all over, inside and out, with matt black paint, which is the sort that doesn't shine when it's dry. (While you've got the black paint out, paint a 1 m length of wire, too.) Wrap the ends of the hooks in silver tape to make them stand out more.

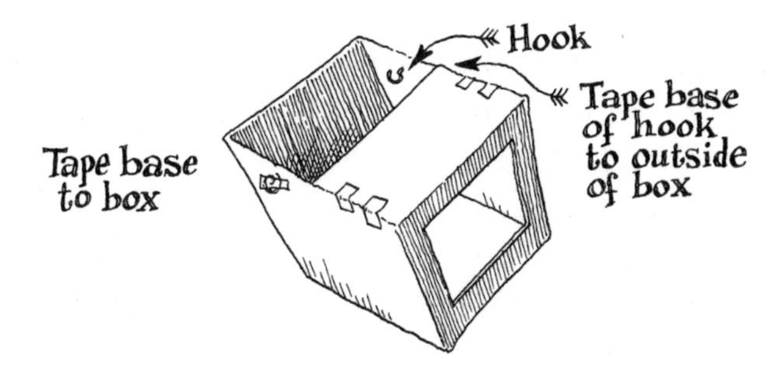


Cut your rope so that it's about 10 cm longer than the distance between the hooks. Put each end of the rope through a keyring, double it over and tape around it to hold it in place. Before fixing the second keyring, check that the rope will be the exact length so that when both keyrings are put on the hooks, the rope is pulled tight across the inside of the box.

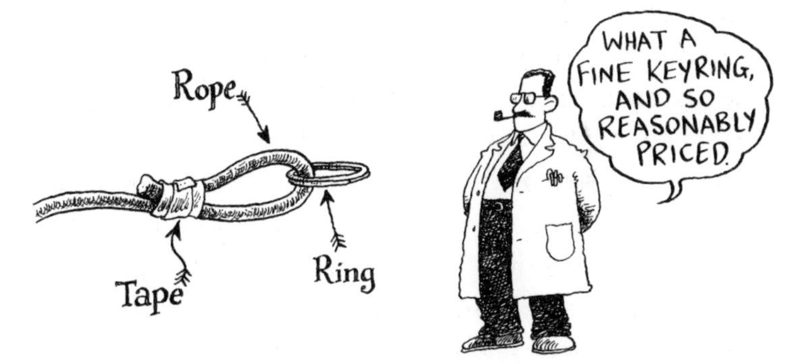


Now take your long piece of black-painted wire and stick about 60 cm of it through the back of the

box, about a quarter of the way from one side and at the same height as the hooks. The piece of wire inside the box should be bent as shown below so that the long end of the wire runs alongside the rope. The piece of wire outside the back of the box should be bent down the back as shown opposite.

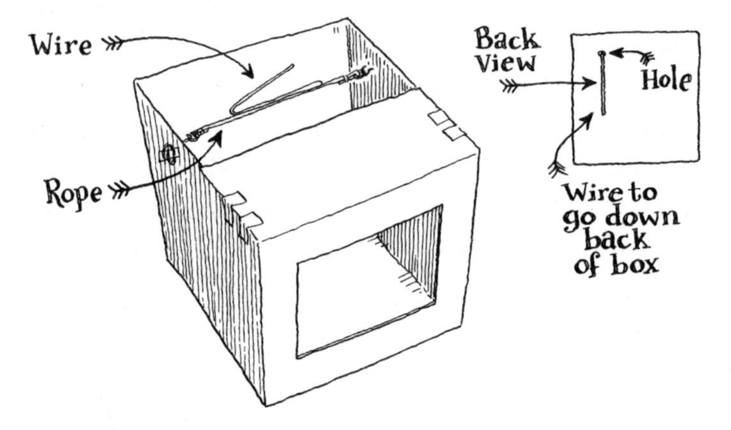


Once the wire has been bent to shape, lightly tape the wire to the rope, then carefully unhook the rope and remove the rope and wire together without unbending the wire. Glue the rope and wire all the way along as firmly as possible, then remove the tape. When the glue is dry, put the wire back in position in the box. To secure the wire, the bottom 2 cm outside the box should be bent in towards the box and then

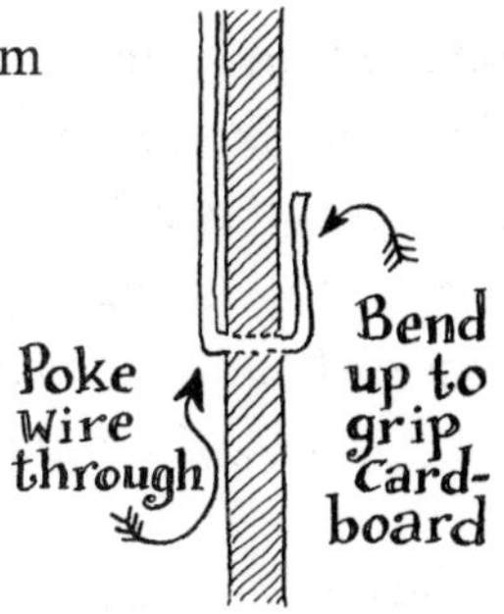


pushed through the cardboard from the back. The tiny piece of wire that comes through to the inside should be bent upwards so it pinches the cardboard tightly. (You might need to lie the box on its back and push the wire end down with pliers.)

When you've finished, from the front of the box it should look as if the centre of the rope is floating with the ends hanging down. The wire should not be visible. Check that you can fasten and unfasten the keyrings on the ends of the rope to the hooks.

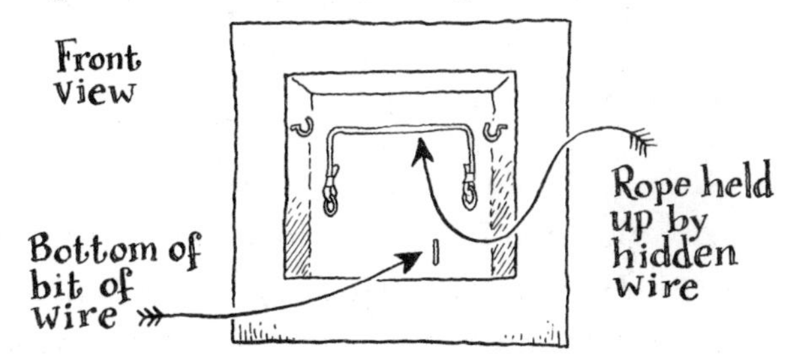


Decorate the box inside and out with stickers – shiny stars are best if you have them. Make sure you put a sticker over the tiny piece of wire sticking in though the back of the box to hide it. Avoid putting any stickers behind where the wire is holding the rope. If you want to be really crafty, stick one of the lid flaps to the back of the box to hide the wire that goes down the outside. Paint this black too.

Finally, you need to make a "solid metal hoop" out of some more stiff wire. Rather than a circle, the best shape for the hoop is a rectangle measuring about 40 cm x 20 cm. Twist the ends of the wire firmly together so that there is no suspicion that you could undo them during the trick. If you have a roll of silver tape, you could wrap it all the way round the rectangle making it look more solid and magical.

**PERFORMANCE**

Make sure your audience can only see in through the front of the box, and start with the rope attached to the hooks.

Borrow some pants, then reach into the box and lie the waistband of the pants over the centre of the rope (where the hidden wire is). While you're doing this, let your volunteer examine the metal hoop. Clip the pants to the rope with the two clothes pegs, being careful not to bend the supporting wire.

Gently undo one end of the rope and then the other letting them dangle down. Now take the hoop and pass it over the pants and wire as shown.

You need to pass the hoop right along the pants and the wire together, then pass it back behind the pants along the wire, then turn it and finally pass it along the pants and off the end. To the audience, it looks like you've just passed the hoop over the pants twice and you've shown there's nothing connecting the pants to the back of the box. Try not to jangle the hoop against the wire.

Finally, reconnect the rope to the hooks, carefully unpeg the pants and return them.

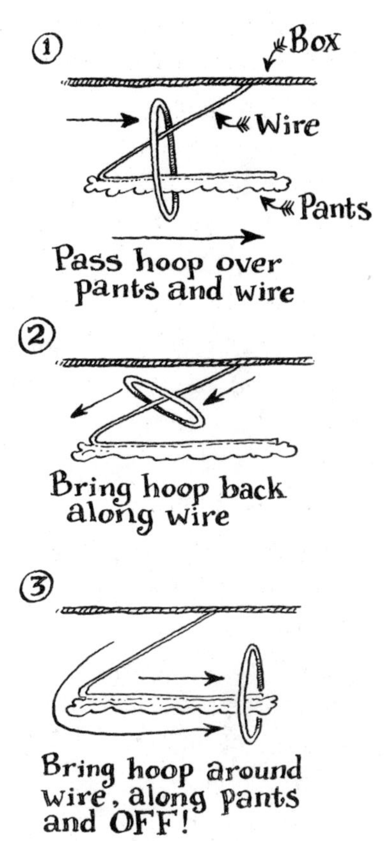


NOTE: The secret of this trick is the contrast between the bright colours of the rope, hooks, stars and hoops, and the dead black colour of the invisible wire. Therefore, when borrowing the pants, try to get a pair that is as bright and colourful as possible.

## The Saucepants

*Upgrade your undies*

The conjuror asks if there is a lady in the audience wearing a dull pair of pants.

When a volunteer presents herself, the conjuror offers to give her pants a makeover. He asks her to remove her pants and pass them to him. "Relax, madam," he announces. "I'm going to take my saucepan and cook you up some Saucepants." He drops the dull pants into an empty saucepan. "Time to add the magic ingredient – sauce powder." He tips up a box of "sauce powder" and some glitter flies out. He sticks the box into the pan. He does a magic gesture, pulls the box away and shows that the dull pants have disappeared. But then he does a final gesture over the pan and...

**PANTSACADABRA!!**

**...he reaches into the pan and pulls out a pair of extremely brightly coloured Saucepants, which he passes to the delighted volunteer.**

WHAT YOU NEED

- A saucepan with a black inside
- A piece of black card
- Some very brightly coloured Saucepants (take a pair of brightly coloured pants and decorate them with extra colour, ribbons and glitter)
- An empty washing-powder box
- A piece of black thread
- Two paper clips
- Some glitter

PREPARATION

You need to prepare the pan by laying your Saucepants flat in the bottom of the pan. Cut a circle from your black card exactly the same size as the bottom of the pan and lie it on top of the pants. Use a piece of tape to make a "hinge" to hold one side of the card in place. From a distance, the card should make the pan look empty.

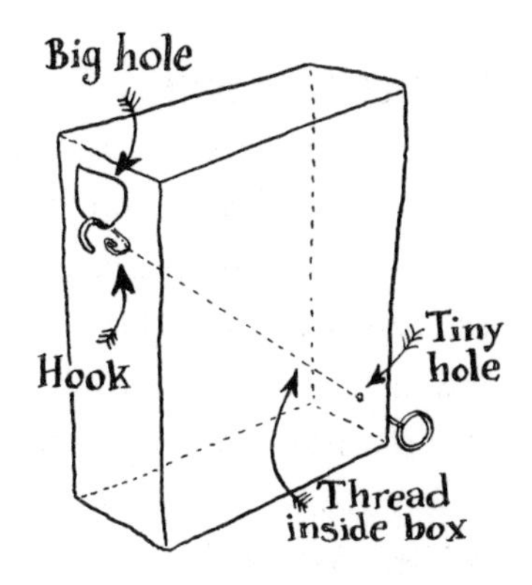


The washing-powder box should have just one hole in the corner where the powder came out. This hole should be big enough to allow the dull pants to slip easily inside it. Decorate the box and write "Sauce Box" on it.

Make a tiny hole in the corner of the box furthest from the big hole. Feed the thread through the tiny hole and bring it out of the big hole. Make a hook out of one of the paper clips and tie it to the end of the thread by the big hole. Hook the thread on to the edge of the hole. Make a ring with the other paper clip just big enough so you can easily slip your finger into it. Tie the ring on the other end of the thread, where it comes out of the tiny hole. (You may like to hide the ring by fixing it to the bottom of the box with a tiny bit of Blu-tack.) Sprinkle some glitter into the box.

**PERFORMANCE**

For this trick, the dull pants you need to borrow should be as small and flimsy as possible, so bear this in mind when selecting your volunteer.

First tip the pan up to show that it is "empty". When tipping the pan, rather than holding the handle, grab the pan on the opposite side to where you stuck the tape hinge. Put your thumb on the outside of the pan and your fingers down the inside so that they can reach the piece of black card and hold it in place. Once the pan is shown, put it back on the table.

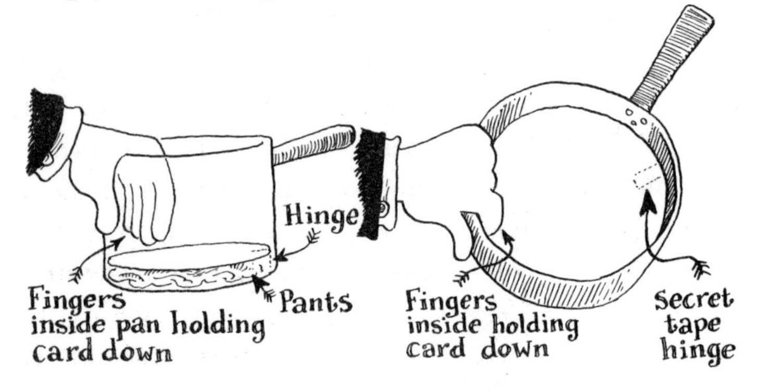


Take the dull pants in your right hand and holding them upside-down by the gusset, drop them into the pan. This should leave the gusset uppermost in the pan. Take the sauce box in your right hand, sprinkle some glitter from the big hole into the pan, then lower the corner of the box with the hole right into the pan. As you do so, pretend to be shaking more glitter into the pan – in reality, you are catching the gusset of the

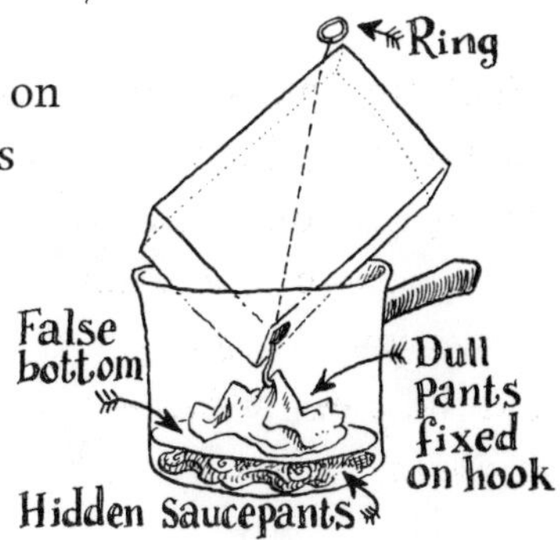


dull pants with the hook on the thread. (If this is tricky, put your left hand in the pan and attach the pants to the hook – pretending that you are mixing the magic ingredients.)

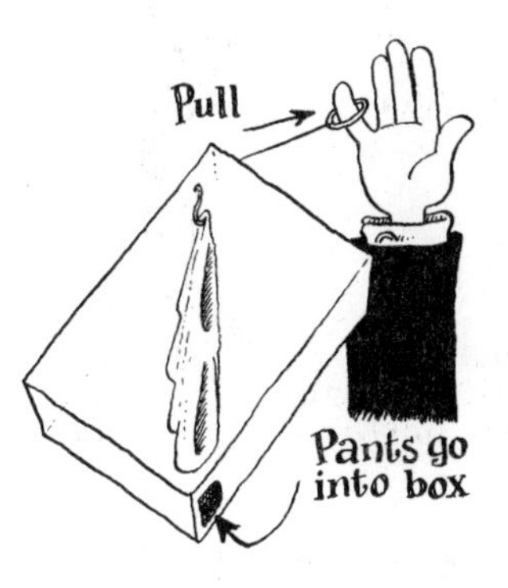


Once the pants are engaged, hold the box in place with your left hand. Wave your right hand as if doing a few magical gestures, but during your final gesture, secretly put your finger in the ring on the thread and pull it. This should cause the pants to disappear up into the box.

Once this is done, grasp the side of the box with your right hand (still with the ring on your finger) and pull it away. Hold the pan with the left hand and show it to be "empty" as before. Discreetly slip the ring off your finger, and slip the ring into the big hole in the box to stop the thread flapping about. While making a final magic gesture, reach into the pan under

the flap, pull out the Saucepants and pass them to your volunteer.

**PANTS PATTER**

Millicent Stitch holds the world record for embroidering the most pants. In a glittering 50-year career she has embroidered thousands of pairs of special pants that have been worn for coronations, film premieres, parliamentary debates and major sporting events. She is credited with being the first person to realize the advertising potential of lady tennis players' underwear.

## The X-ray Photopants Frame

*A forceful miracle*

The audience is shown an empty photo frame. The conjuror explains that the photo frame has the magic ability to take X-ray pictures and shows what people look like when they are only wearing a pair of pants. He covers the photo frame with a cloth and sets it to one side.

He then invites a spectator on stage and offers her three pairs of pants to choose from. Once a pair has been selected and the other two discarded, the conjuror holds the pants across his middle and asks, "Would you like to see what I look like in these pants?" Once the cheers have died down, to everyone's amazement he whisks the cloth from the photo frame and...

**PANTSACADABRA!!**

**...in the frame a picture has appeared of the conjuror wearing the selected pants.**

**WHAT YOU NEED**

- Three pairs of different-coloured pants
- A photo frame – one of those ones with a piece of glass at the front held on to a backboard with metal clips is best
- A photo (or funny drawing) of yourself wearing one of the pairs of pants. It should be smaller than the frame and cut out to shape.
- Two bits of identical black silk (or other thin fabric) slightly larger than the frame
- A large black cloth
- Glue, scissors

## PREPARATION

Take the photo frame apart, then cover the backboard with one of the bits of silk, folding the edges of the silk around the back of the board all the way. Glue the silk firmly into position so that it can't slip. Next glue your photo or picture to the silk-covered board, taking care that all the edges are fixed down firmly. Remember, your picture should be a cut-out and so there should be some of the background silk visible. Make sure the glue is absolutely dry before continuing.

Cut the second piece of silk to the exact size of the glass, apart from an extra tag sticking out at one corner. Position the second piece of silk exactly over the picture, and then place the glass on top. Fix the glass in place with the metal clips, but leave the extra tag of silk sticking out. The tag should be folded down behind the frame out of view. The photo frame will now appear to be empty, but when you pull on the tag, the loose silk should slide out revealing the picture. (Try it – and if the loose silk doesn't pull out easily, take off the metal clip nearest to it and then prise the clip slightly further open with some pliers. Put the clip back on and try again. Once you're happy it works, undo the clips, replace the loose silk, fix it all back up again and you're ready.)

**PERFORMANCE**

Show the "empty" photo frame, then cover it with the black cloth. Invite your volunteer to the stage, show the three pairs of pants and "force" the correct pair. (See page 33 for *Forcing Your Pants*) Finally, reach for the covered frame. When you're ready to remove the cloth, grab it with your finger and thumb at the corner of the frame where the loose tag of silk is. That way you should also be able to grab the loose tag, so when you pull away the cloth, the silk will slide out from the frame revealing your picture. While everyone is gasping at the picture, bundle the cloth up so that the loose bit of silk doesn't fall out.

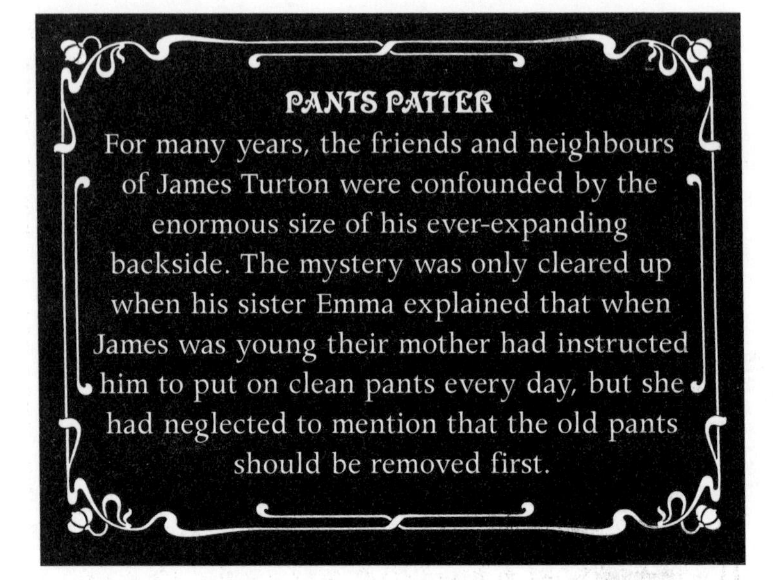
PANTS PATTER
For many years, the friends and neighbours of James Turton were confounded by the enormous size of his ever-expanding backside. The mystery was only cleared up when his sister Emma explained that when James was young their mother had instructed him to put on clean pants every day, but she had neglected to mention that the old pants should be removed first.

# Showstoppers

*The final three tricks are major dramatic set pieces and require the use of designers, stage technicians, costumed assistants... and money.*

## The Genie of the Pants

*A quick rub and the genie appears*

This was probably the finest illusion that the Great Gusset performed at the Palace of Grand Thong. The conjuror himself was dressed up to play the part of the Chinese laundry boy, and he also called upon the services of Cringe the butler and Dennis the elephant scrubber to be the uncle and the genie. Here are all the details of the trick as the audience saw it...

NO! AND FOR YOUR FOOLISHNESS YOU SHALL NOW DIE! MWAH HA HA HARR!
SPLATCH
SLAM!
UGH! THEY'RE FILTHY! MAY AS WELL GIVE THEM A WASH...
SPLISH SPLOSH
BAH! THERE'S STILL A MARK ON THEM. I'LL JUST RUB IT OFF...
PANTSACADABRA!!
GASP!
I AM THE GENIE OF THE PANTS. YOUR WISH IS MY COMMAND!

**THE SECRET**

At last, the secret of how a real live disembodied head appeared from a pair of pants can be revealed. The diagram tells all:

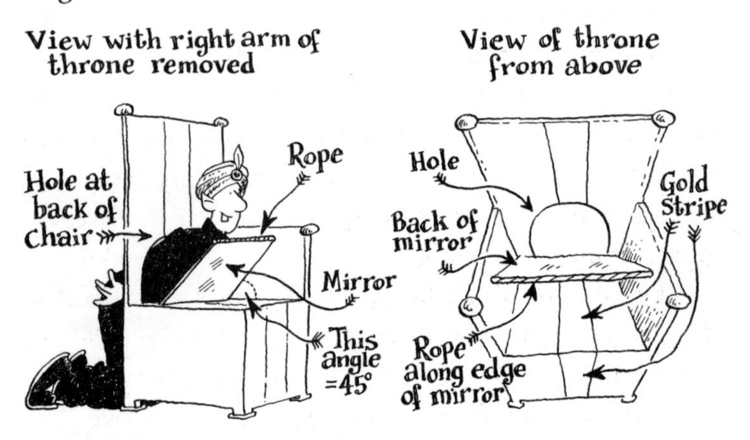


Right from the start there is a piece of brightly coloured rope hanging between the arms of the throne on to which the pants are hung. However the main purpose of the rope is to disguise the top of an angled mirror which is fitted between the arms of the throne. The audience are quite unaware of this mirror, and when they look from the front, they think they can see the whole of the back of the throne. In fact what they see below the rope is the reflection of the seat of the throne. This allows for a hole to be made in the

lower part of the back of the throne, so "the genie" can slide through and put his head on top of the rope. This way the body seems invisible, but the head can be clearly seen.

The throne should be painted in a single dark colour, and then, to make the illusion more convincing, a thick gold stripe can be painted up the centre of the front, seat and back of the throne. When the throne is viewed from the front, the mirror will make the stripe look continuous, even if an observer moves from side to side.

The trick needs to be performed on a stage so that the seat of the throne is about level with the heads of the audience. To create the perfect illusion, the lighting should come from spotlights above the audience. The audience needs to be arranged at least 10 m back from the throne, and gathered directly in front of it. The rear of the stage should be black and, apart from the head, the assistant playing the genie should be dressed completely in black.

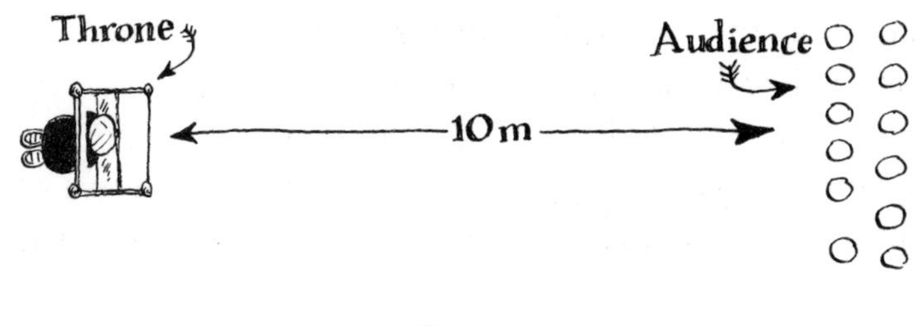

Prior to performance, the pants and clothes pegs can be draped over the back of the chair but they should not be placed on the seat. Otherwise, the audience will see the reflection of the pegs and pants in the mirror.

When the Great Gusset presented this illusion at the palace, at first people thought that the head wasn't real.

But then, once the Empress was convinced that the head was genuine, it led to even further complications.

## PANTS PATTER

Some years ago, the army developed special pairs of camouflaged pants to go with the rest of their camouflage outfits. Sadly, these were not a success because, after several weeks, even though the wearers were invisible they could always be detected by the smell. As one soldier explained, "these camouflage pants are fine when you put them on, but when you need to take them off and wash them, you can't find them."

# The Bride of Pantenstein

*An enactment of a gothic tale*

In the centre of the stage there are two trestles across which a large box will be laid. To the side of the stage there is a large control box covered in dials and switches, to which two heavy cables may be connected.

Doctor Pantenstein enters the stage. He hangs a chart on the wall showing a life-size diagram of the humanoid creature he hopes to create. On his command, two assistants carry a sarcophagus on stage and place it on the two trestles. The sarcophagus is tipped on to its side and the lid opened to show that it is empty.

The doctor wipes around the inside with a cloth to convince the audience that there is nothing there. The lid is replaced and the sarcophagus tipped back upright.

The doctor opens a selection of bags, boxes and suitcases and takes out a selection of body parts. The lid of the sarcophagus is opened while the doctor consults the diagram, then the body parts are laid inside along with a set of bride's clothing. When the final piece of clothing has been put in, the doctor chants: "Come to life, my beauty! Come to life!"

Sadly, nothing happens. The doctor is distraught, but then has an idea. His assistants are sent off stage, and then return. One has two massive electric cables, the other has a large pair of pants. The ends of the cables are connected to the control box and the other ends to the pants. The pants are lowered into the sarcophagus and the lid is closed.

The doctor then mutters a silent prayer and operates the switches and levers on the control box.

The assistants step back hurriedly from the sarcophagus as the lid starts to twitch. Suddenly the lid flies open and...

**...the living bride of Pantenstein sits up and steps out of the sarcophagus wearing the pants – which have lit up.**

**WHAT YOU NEED**

- Three assistants – two to carry the sarcophagus and one small female assistant to be the "bride"
- The sarcophagus (see "Preparation" opposite)
- Two trestles to stand the sarcophagus on
- Two identical large pairs of pants
- A box with lots of dials and switches
- Two long wires with clips on the end
- Two sets of white bride outfits
- Spare body parts (these should be false)
- A set of battery-operated Christmas lights

**PREPARATION**

This trick should be performed with the audience arranged towards the front. The secret lies in the contruction of the "sarcophagus". There are three basic pieces that are hinged together as shown in the diagram.

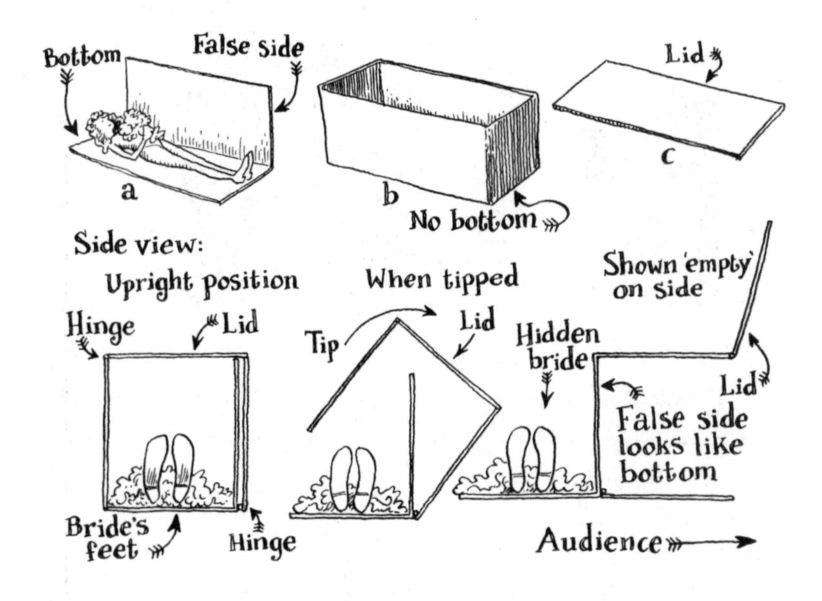


Part (a) should fit exactly into part (b), and is then hinged along the bottom. In this way, part (b) can be tipped on its side leaving the bottom still lying flat. When the audience sees the false side, everyone will

assume that it is the bottom of the box. The lid (c) is closed during the tipping so that the audience does not see that the false side remains upright.

The insides of the box should all be loosely covered with black sheets of cloth to give the impression of a silk-lined casket. However, there should be an extra loose cloth on the bottom of the box under which the bride can cover herself while the box is being tipped. This will ensure that nobody accidentally catches a glimpse of her.

Take one pair of the pants, make lots of little holes in them and poke the Christmas lights through. Arrange for the switch for the lights to be in a position where the bride can operate it.

The bride should be dressed in bride's clothes with the wired up pants on the outside. Before the show, the bride should be lying in the box with the extra black cloth over her.

**PERFORMANCE**

When your assistants carry the sarcophagus in, they should put it down towards the rear of the trestles, thus allowing enough space to tip it over.

When the assistants tip the box over and open the lid, make a point of reaching right inside to show it is

empty. Walk right around it, even banging the false side from the back, but when you walk behind the box, avoid looking at the bride. Then the assistants close the lid and set the box upright.

Collect the body parts and check the diagram as the assistants open the lid again. By this time the bride should have pushed the cloth aside. As you put the body parts in the box, she can hide them under the cloth.

When the assistants bring on the wire and the (unwired) pants, clip the wires to the pants and put them in the box. When the lid is closed, the bride unclips the wires and transfers them to her own pants and switches the lights on. She hides the unwired pair of pants under the black cloth.

These instructions only explain the basic mechanics of the trick – the fine details of the performance are left to the individual.

NOTE: If it is desired to capitalize on the gruesome aspect of the spectacle, the dress worn by the bride could be ripped and made to look bloody. The bride herself could have make-up scars across her neck, shoulders and knees to indicate that she was formed from separate pieces.

## The Grand Musical Finale

*A truly magnificent spectacle*

The orchestra plays the introduction as the conjuror comes on and proceeds to sing...

### The biggest pair of panties in the world

*It's the biggest pair of panties in the world*
*The finest fold of fabric ever unfurled*
*Hold them to your nose, they dangle*
*round your feet*
*Pull them to the side and they stretch*
*across the street*
*My top cheeks are rosy,*
*My bottom cheeks are cosy*
*For while they're on my nethers'll never be curl'd.*
*It's the pride of pioneering*
*elastic engineering,*
*it's the biggest pair of panties in the world!*

As he starts singing, the conjuror reaches into his waistband and pulls up the bright red side twangs of his pants, to the point where he can hook them on to his shoulders like braces. He then raises his leg and an assistant reaches a hand up inside his trousers and pulls out the bottom part of the gusset. The gusset is eased over the conjuror's foot, then two further assistants pull upwards on the side twangs so that the large pair of pants slide freely up the conjuror's body, out of his trousers and right off over his head.

The conjuror leaves the stage as the assistants stretch out the pants to show their size, then bundle them into a washing machine. The pants spin round, the assistants reach in, pull them out – and stretch them out, whereupon they are twice the size. The pants are then put through a giant mangle – when they emerge they are even bigger again!

The pants are then hauled into a laundry basket, which is taken to the back of the stage. Two cables are lowered from the roof and attached to the pants, the cables are tightened and the pants are pulled up, covering the entire back wall of the stage. The pants start to wobble and shake, then the conjuror's head and shoulders appear through the convenience hole and a chorus line of singers pops up over the waistband.

PEXTON'S
LAUNDRY

PANTSACADABRA!

A final chorus is sung as fireworks go off.

*It's the biggest pair of panties in the world*
*The finest fold of fabric ever unfurled*
*Use them as a tent, to keep you fit and hearty*
*Invite along your friends*
*there's room to throw a party*
*Twang that elastic*
*The power's so fantastic*
*That off to outer space they will be hurled*
*But still they'll entertain us*
*When we see them on Uranus*
*It's the biggest pair...*
*The biggest pair...*
*The biggest pair of panties in the world!*

**WHAT YOU NEED**

- You need four pairs of pants in different sizes listed here as (a), (b), (c) and (d): (a): a very big pair of red pants (waistband about 1 m-wide unstretched); (b): an enormously large pair of red pants (waistband about 4 m unstretched); (c): a magnificently massive pair of red pants (waistband about 10 m unstretched); (d): a colossally gigantic pair of red pants (waistband should be over 25 m and made from reinforced steel cable). There should be a door flap in the back of these pants and internal rope ladders leading up to the waistband.
- A large pretend washing-machine
- A very large pretend mangle
- A huge laundry basket
- Two cable winches and around 100 m of steel cable
- A very high stepladder
- Two assistants
- Orchestra and chorus singers
- Trousers with an elasticated waistband

**PREPARATION**

This trick should be performed in a massive arena. The back of the stage should be masked by a giant pair of curtains. The stepladders should be in position behind the curtains. There should be a trapdoor in the

floor by the centre of these curtains. Pants (d) should be hidden down this trapdoor with the side twangs on top so that cables may be easily attached. The laundry basket should be positioned immediately in front of the trapdoor, with the hinge of the lid towards the back of the stage.

A cable winch should be set to either side of the stage, and the cables draped over high pulleys.

The mangle should be positioned to one side of the stage with pants (c) secreted behind it.

The washing-machine should be set to the other side of the stage with pants (b) already tucked inside the drum out of view.

You should be wearing pants (a) underneath your trousers with the elasticated waistband. Ensure the gusset is fed right down one of your trouser legs and tucked into your sock.

Before the trick, the chorus singers should be waiting behind curtains at the foot of the stepladder.

**PERFORMANCE**

Sing the first verse of the song, then pull the side twangs of the red pants up and stick your arms through them, so easing them on to your shoulders. Call on your assistants, one of whom takes the gusset

from your sock, pulls it clear of your trouser leg and passes it over your foot. Then the side twangs are taken by the assistants and pulled up. At this point, you will have both legs in the same leg hole, so the pants will slide right up your body, slip free of your elasticated trousers and may be pulled off over your head. The pants are then bundled into the very back of the washing machine. Now you leave the stage and make your way round behind the curtains to the stepladder.

Meanwhile, the assistants close the washing-machine door, allow the drum to rotate a few times, then open the door and pull out pants (b). These are spread out and displayed, then taken round to the back of the mangle. As the mangle is turned, pants (b) are allowed to fall out of sight, but instead pants (c) are fed through the rollers from behind. Once clear, pants (c) are spread out for display.

Pants (c) are then packed into the laundry basket and the lid is closed. The basket is rotated so that the hinge is towards the audience, and the lid opened. The cables are lowered and the assistants connect them to the side twangs of pants (d). The cables are raised, spreading the pants across the back of the stage. Once in position, you climb the stepladder and sneak through the curtains, and into the pants via the

doorflap. You may then appear through the convenience hole and sing the final chorus of the song.

As you do so, the chorus singers climb the stepladder and enter the pants, then climb the rope ladder to take position along the waistband.

NOTES: The lid of the laundry basket should only open to an upright position, and not be allowed to fall all the way back. Otherwise the audience may notice that the pants being hoisted up by the cables are not the same pair as those that came through the mangle.

Hear "The Biggest Pair of Panties in The World" performed at www.magicofpants.co.uk.

# The Great Gusset's Spantacular Curtain Call

Once you've performed "The Biggest Pair of Panties in the World" you can rest assured that you've taken *The Magic of Pants* as far as it can go. Bear in mind that the tricks that you have mastered over the past 217 pages were inspired by that first performance all those years ago by the Great Gusset and since then they have been

developed and refined to maximize the magic and eliminate danger. Therefore, it's time to retire and savour your glorious memories. Above all, you must resist the temptation to push back the frontiers of pant-antics any further.

Sadly, this advice comes too late for the Great Gusset. After the success of his appearance before the Empress he took himself on tour around the world presenting ever-more stunning pant illusions and miracles. But, tragically, his quest for extreme underwear entertainment was to be his undoing. The public appetite for pant excitement was becoming harder and harder to satisfy, and so having exhausted trickery he turned his talents towards death-defying undie stunts. In the end it was his *Ultimate Pants Plunge* that lead to his untimely death.

It was a clear April morning when a crowd was gathered on the very edge of a high clifftop to witness the conjuror wearing nothing but a vest. Far, far below him pegged out on a line strung above the rocks was a pair of industrial-strength pants. The challenge was simple – Gusset planned to leap from the cliff feet first and land safely in the pants. Of course, if his feet missed the leg holes by just so much as a toe width, he would be splattered across the unforgiving rocks.

The wind was right, visibility was perfect and the pants were washed and ready. The crowd held its breath as, with a final wave, he leapt from the cliff. Whether or not he had prepared some secret method to ensure the

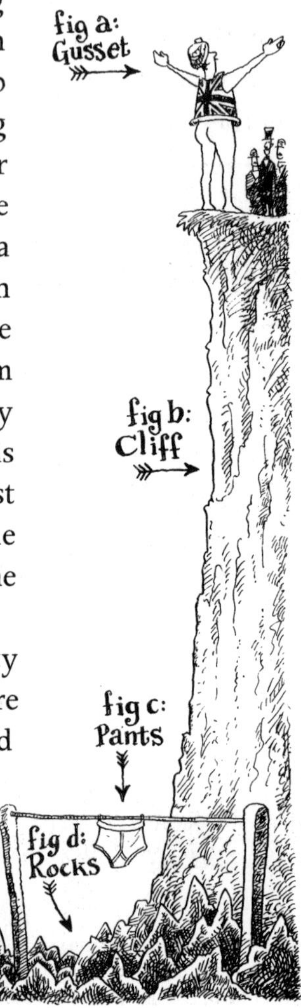

stunt would pass off safely will never be known, but the one factor he could not have accounted for was that at the precise moment of his descent, his mother would be passing underneath.

And thus ended the legend that was the Great Gusset. He died as he had lived – investigating the mysteries of the most popular item of clothing ever worn. Therefore, friends, when we look back on his life, be grateful for his guidance and remember the joy he brought us with a smile. He wouldn't want us to weep or wail, he'd just want to be remembered as the man who introduced the world to … *The Magic of Pants.*